M000310625

WITH MUCH FIRE
IN THE HEART

THE LETTERS OF
MOHAMMED MRABET

TO

IRVING STETTNER

TRANSLATED BY

PAUL BOWLES

First edition
after the printing of limited
editions totaling one hundred copies.

———————————————

WITH MUCH FIRE IN THE HEART

THE LETTERS OF
MOHAMMED MRABET

TO

IRVING STETTNER

TRANSLATED BY

PAUL BOWLES

First Edition
Printed on acid-free paper
Published by Lightning Source
An INGRAM Company
La Vergne, Tennessee, USA
Kiln Farm, Milton Keynes, UK

Copyright © 2011 Ronald J. Papandrea
All rights reserved

LCCN: 2009903859

Paperback ISBN: 978-0-9746527-5-7

Paperback Retail Price: $19.99 USD, £12.99 GBP, €14.99 EUR

Hardcover Retail Price: $29.99 USD, £19.99 GBP, €22.99 EUR

Hardcover ISBN: 978-0-9746527-6-4

**Available from all major English language book distributors
with 55% wholesale discount and returns accepted.**

This book is dedicated to Irving Stettner (1922-2004):

the gold light of day
is only there to make way
for the silver night

la lumière d'or du jour
est seulement là pour ouvrir la voie
pour la nuit argentée

in the walled city
wandering, I found a place
where I lost my self

dans la ville murée
errant, j'ai trouvé un endroit
où j'ai perdu mon être

there is a dance room
in a Tangier hotel; now
the drum is beating

il y a une salle de danse
dans un hôtel de Tanger; maintenant
le tambour bat

"I was delighted to receive your wonderful letter today. I am replying immediately. The fact that you can not read has perhaps made you a better writer than most who do read."

Henry Miller to Mohammed Mrabet
June 7, 1979[1]

"I've been corresponding with Irving Stettner for several years. Everyone tells me he is a delightful man. Mrabet does write him letters. I don't "ghostwrite" them; I merely translate them as he dictates."

Paul Bowles
April 23, 1983[2]

---

[1] Letter from Henry Miller to Mohammed Mrabet, dated June 7, 1979, Henry Miller, *From Your Capricorn Friend, Henry Miller and the Stroker, 1978-1980*, Forward by Irving Stettner, 1984 (New Directions Publishing Corporation, N.Y.C.), page 60. Henry Miller (1891-1980) was the famed author of *Tropic of Cancer, Tropic of Capricorn* and other autobiographical novels.

[2] Letter from Paul Bowles to Joel Redon, dated April 23, 1983, Paul Bowles, *In Touch: The Letters of Paul Bowles*, edited by Jeffrey Miller, 1994 (Farrar, Straus and Giroux), page 517. Paul Bowles (1910-1999) was a writer and composer who lived most of his life in Tangier, Morocco. He is best known for *The Sheltering Sky*, published in 1949.

Introductory Note

On June 4, 1988, Irving Stettner and I were in Lyon, France, for the opening of his one-man watercolor show. We soon left for Morocco to meet Mohammed Mrabet and Paul Bowles. Irving and I discussed the possibility of publishing Mrabet's letters. Mrabet had tape recorded the letters in Moghrebi (Moroccan spoken Arabic) and Paul Bowles had translated them into English. Irving had previously published them in his magazine, *Stroker*; but I thought they deserved a wider audience. While in Tangier, I obtained approval from Mrabet and Bowles to publish the letters. In 1989, Irving wrote a forward and sent it to me. Other Stroker Press projects intervened to delay the planned book. Irving Stettner died the early morning of January 16, 2004. This book is our last project together. The title was chosen by Irving from a suggestion of his friend, Karl Orend, the owner of Alyscamps Press. It is taken from Mrabet's letter of June 17, 1980, to Tommy Trantino, published in *Stroker 17*. Mrabet ended this letter:

Adios, hasta Dios quiere. (Good-bye, until God wants it)
with much luck and power, and much fire
in the heart.

Ron Papandrea
November 7, 2004

Irving Stettner, Ron Papandrea, Mohammed Mrabet and Paul Bowles,
in Paul Bowles' apartment, Tangier, Morocco, June, 1988.
(Photograph credit: Carina Blomback/Merwi Andelin)
(*Stroker 40*, inside cover)

Ink Drawing by Mohammed Mrabet, Cover of *Stroker 13*.

Ink Drawing by Mohammed Mrabet, Cover of *Stroker 23*.

Ink Drawing by Mohammed Mrabet, *Stroker 16*, page 33.

Ink Drawing by Mohammed Mrabet, *Stroker 16*, page 28.

Mohammed Mrabet
(Background: Ketama, the cannabis center of North Africa)
(*Stroker 14*, page 13)

Mohammed Mrabet
(*Stroker 16*, page 37)

Irving Stettner, Mohammed Mrabet and Paul Bowles,
in Paul Bowles' apartment, Tangier, Morocco, June, 1988.
(Photograph by Ron Papandrea)

Mohammed Mrabet, in Paul Bowles' apartment,
Tangier, Morocco, June, 1988.
(Photograph by Ron Papandrea)

Mrabet's farm house,
near Tangier, Morocco, July, 1988.
(Photograph by Ron Papandrea)

Mrabet with son, at Mrabet's farm,
near Tangier, Morocco, July, 1988.
(Photograph by Ron Papandrea)

Mohammed Mrabet and friends, at Mrabet's farm,
near Tangier, Morocco, July, 1988.
(Photograph by Ron Papandrea)

Inside Mrabet's farm house,
near Tangier, Morocco, July, 1988.
(Photograph by Ron Papandrea)

Inside Mrabet's farm house,
near Tangier, Morocco, July, 1988.
(Photograph by Ron Papandrea)

Inside Mrabet's farm house,
near Tangier, Morocco, July, 1988.
(Photograph by Ron Papandrea)

Leaving Mrabet's farm,
near Tangier, Morocco, July, 1988.
(Photograph by Ron Papandrea)

Leaving Mrabet's farm,
near Tangier, Morocco, July, 1988.
(Photograph by Ron Papandrea)

CONTENTS

Letter from Mohammed Mrabet to Tommy Trantino:

Letters from Mohammed Mrabet to Irving Stettner:

---

[3] The date is incorrectly given in *Stroker 26-27* and in the *Stroker Anthology 1974-1994*, edited by Irving Stettner, 1994 (Stroker Press, Ron Papandrea & Robert Schumann).

FORWARD BY IRVING STETTNER

REALLY THE MAN largely responsible for this book was no other than Henry Miller. Yes, believe it or not!

In February, 1978[4], Henry Miller began contributing to my magazine <u>Stroker</u> -- sending letters, original essays, short stories, etc. -- we were corresponding hotly. This continued until a couple of months before Henry left this earthly realm on June 7, 1980. In his letters he was always raving about some writer or artist, recommending them strongly. Though they were seldom living, contemporary ones, I noticed.

Till one day he wrote me wildly about a new, strange writer coming out of North Africa -- Tangier, Morocco, more exactly -- one by the name of Mohammed Mrabet. A friend-fan of his in Salt Lake City, Pat Eddington, had just sent him Mrabet's autobiographical novel, "Look and Move On". A little later Miller mailed it to me, and in an accompanying letter said: "What a kick I got out of that little book! So simple, so direct, so uncompromising. A real natural."[5]

And it was Miller, in another epistle shortly afterward, who suggested I write Mrabet and ask him to contribute to my magazine.[6] Which I did, and hence this volume of marvelous letters; forty in total, all originally sent by Mohammed Mrabet and duly printed in various issues of <u>Stroker</u>, from Summer 1979 to Fall 1986, a seven year period.

Letters? Yes, and the most precious I've ever received in my life! Finding one in my mailbox, I recall, really made my day. Like manna fallen from above. Or sheer jewels, and almost literally, beginning with the fragile, thin paper, the featherweight light blue envelopes with their large, Arabic-lettered, colorful Moroccan stamps. "Querido Amigo Stettner: I salute you with two hands, and three or four arms." Yes, I'd chuckle, or commiserate, weep, sigh, marvel, gasp for wonder, or belly laugh, or suddenly reading one of Mrabet's inimitable, magical fairy tales, simply jump my skin. Totally bewitched I was, in other words, enchanted, enthralled. It was like receiving a letter from the spirits of Lewis Carroll,

---

[4] Letter from Henry Miller to Irving Stettner, dated 2/24/1978, *Stroker 26-27*, Double Issue, page 46.

[5] Letter from Henry Miller to Irving Stettner, dated December 21, 1978, Henry Miller, *From Your Capricorn Friend, Henry Miller and the Stroker, 1978-1980*, Forward by Irving Stettner, 1984 (New Directions Publishing Corporation, N.Y.C.), page 41.

[6] Letter from Henry Miller to Irving Stettner, dated 6/29/1979, <u>Stroker</u> 21, page 4.

Vaslav Nijinsky, Antonin Artaud, and the last great Zen monks of Kamakura, all wrapped in one.

Moreover, completely uneducated, Mohammed Mrabet was unable to read or write, I was informed. His letters arrived, or only existed because they had been translated into English by Paul Bowles, the well-known American writer and composer living in Tangier (since 1947). From age 11 in the streets and fending for himself, working as a fishermen's helper, toilet unblocker, kif pusher and even a bouncer in a brothel, Mrabet writes with a firm grasp on reality, life and the world.

"Amigo Stettner, I'm not a writer", as he says in one letter, "… because I can't read or write. But ever since I was little I've been with fantastic people and seen fantastic things." He writes out of a superabundance, an overflowing cornucopia of experiences, encounters, deprivations, joys. Why at times he writes so deliriously, rapturously, even inanely! And -- yes, why he can nourish us with so many precious kernels of wisdom.

There is a parallel with Maxim Gorki (also Francois Villon, Whitman, Jack Kerouac), who in his early youth was a vagabond, tramped and worked all over Russia for his apprenticeship, "universities of life". And there is another similarity: both, despite bitter experiences, hardships, ended up with a smiling, granite optimism: "Amigo Stettner, everything is good. Everything that happens to a man during his life, bad or good, he must make good by giving thanks for being alive. I always say everything is good."

Letter writing, beginning with the amatory exchange between Heloise and Abelard, has always been a recognized literary form. In the pages which follow it has been experimented with, assuredly; or expanded to the nth degree -- or simply smashed to smithereens. Since if Mrabet begins an epistle in a warm, friendly tone, nota bene any moment he will jag off into a lengthy fable, folk tale, parable, pastoral poem or two, eclogue, trenchant elegy, jeremiad, a riff of pure Surrealist automatic writing, and -- suddenly drop a gelignite bomb or two into our lap. Later whenever he waxes irascible, angry, or relating some incident, anecdote which includes a few harsh, brutal details, he won't hesitate to mention them. He accepts life, in all its aspects. Hence often the sharp, barbed, veracious ring to his words.

Replete with ichors, blue snapdragons, stardust, he has a streak of the poet in him a mile-wide. And perhaps why he has so many misadventures, pratfalls, loses out in marital imbroglios, etc. ("The clown is the poet in action", Henry Miller.) Though his forte is the art of storytelling, at which he is a consummate master. Natural to him as breathing. If Paul Bowles wasn't around to translate his tales, he'd probably be telling them to a group of his buddies at the nearest café, over a cup of mint tea, and a pipe full of kif. Undoubtedly born with an overdose of imagination (luckily for us!), he just has to exercise it, or bust. All he really needs in life is a few patient, attentive ears to hear him out, or let him wave his magic wand.

True, there are times when Mohammed complains, laments, groans, moans, waves the crying towel. Is it just part of his "act"? Or his great candor? Whatever, it just seems to endear him to us; revealing himself as a simple human being. Meanwhile all of us today who read newspaper headlines, pay taxes, so on -- or who are out in the world to any degree, willy-nilly, caught up in the treadmill, trapped in the modern debacle -- aren't we also ridden with neurosis, petty phobias, fears? And when Mrabet gives expression to them, and in his own unique, naïve fashion -- which is not without a certain charm, admittedly! -- doesn't he help us identify with our own?

But he is contradiction, paradox, multifaceted; the gamut of his emotions almost endless. With each new letter we get another sparkling gem of telluric wisdom, wit and laughter. Mrabet speaks through one of his characters, "… my friend, a man is priceless." Yes, which is another way of saying: "he is endless." Tapping his instincts, intuitions, or abiding his habit of "… writing from inside (his) heart", as he confesses, he has a unique, inexhaustible, precious mine lode, certes. And why what Mrabet delivers is always the pure vein, the grist, the real McCoy.

Also he is not afraid of violence. Yes, a decidedly un-European quality. Violence; Mrabet is unafraid in its presence, or to utilize it. Perhaps he even endows it with a certain purity; anyhow, he simply acts, period. Well-aware of his own imperfections, he knows he is his own worst enemy. Still, he has others: the powerful, the arrogant, the academics, the know-it-alls, the cold bureaucrats, the heartless governments, the cunning politicians. "Things that a poor man can do, a rich man can't do", as he says in one letter. "And whatever a rich man can do, so can a poor man. We're more alive and stronger, and braver in our minds, we poor men. A pure heart is the important thing for me. And nobody knows what is going to happen later on."

Yes, here is a strong voice coming out of North Africa and the whole Arab world. And when Mrabet speaks, doesn't he also do it for his kin, blood and otherwise; the poverty-stricken millions. "And nobody knows what is going to happen later on." Yes, implicit in these words is a threat. And if the rulers of the world ever get to read them … would they tremble in their boots?

"Yes", I would say.

Why? "My friend, a man is priceless."

Irving Stettner
7.22.89

Irving Stettner
129-2nd Avenue #3,
New York, NY 10003

Publisher's Note

The punctuation in Mrabet's letters is the same as when they were first published by Irving Stettner in *Stroker* magazine. Only obvious spelling mistakes and typographical errors have been corrected. Some words are spelled one way in American English and another way in British English. I retained the spelling as published in *Stroker*; the same word may be spelled one way on one page and another way on another page.

(Stroker 21, page 5)   Tangier, Morocco
                                                14 June 1979

Querido Amigo Miller:[7]

I send you many salutations and embraces.

Today, Thursday the fourteenth of June, I went in the morning to visit my mother, and she gave me the letter from you, and I was extremely happy, so happy that I stayed for a moment merely looking at it, and my mother said: What's the matter? Is there some bad news in that letter? No, mother. The opposite. It's a fantastic letter. From a great friend of mine. He doesn't know me, and I don't know him, but he wrote to me. And I write to him because he's a really good man. My mother said: Well, son, God is helping him, and He is helping you. Then I read the letter. It's not necessary for me to say again how happy it made me. And I thank you for all you said in the letter.

Amigo Miller, I showed your first letter to some Europeans here in Tangier. These people had never shown any respect for me, but when they saw the letter, they became different people. If I should show them your second letter, they would explode. Amigo Miller, I'm doing the translation of a new novel which I think will be called <u>Night Honey</u>. And I make a few drawings. This very night I'm going to make one and send it to you.

Amigo Miller, I'm going to tell you something I heard from a very good friend, and not long ago. Only four or five days. He's very old, and he has been blind for many years. He used to be a great fisherman. He said: A man went to the house of another and knocked on the door. The other man came out.

Please, could you lend me your qadra? (That's a big jar made of clay.) The other man said: Yes. Why not? And gave him that jar. Thank you. The other went away with the jar and kept it for a month in his house.

One afternoon he came back to see his friend carrying a jar of the same shape, but much smaller. He knocked on the door, and the other came out. Good afternoon, and hello.

---

[7] Henry Miller (1891-1980), author of numerous works, including *Tropic of Cancer* (1934) and *Tropic of Capricorn* (1939).

Here's a little jar that was just born, said the man. The other stared at him.

The mother's still at my house, but I'll bring her next week, he said.

The next week he came again with another little jar in his hand. Hello, my friend, and how are you? Thanks to Allah, yes, yes.

What's that? said the other.

It's another little one, the same as the first.

And where's the mother?

She's at home with me. I'll bring her tomorrow or the next day, he told him. Good-bye. Good-bye.

Two or three days later he came back again. He knocked and the other came out. What's wrong today? You look sad.

Yes, said the man. The jar is dead.

The owner cried: What do you mean, it's dead?

The poor jar died in childbirth.

Amigo Miller, this is just a joke. I'd like to see you, face to face; I'd like that very much. It's too bad. I can't. I can't have a passport. Because anybody who writes books is a criminal. And I write books. It doesn't matter. Thanks to God I'm a man, because when my father threw me out, and I was ten years old, I slept in the street and was never afraid. One night I was sitting under a tree and the sky was very clear and full of stars. It was cold, and I was looking at the sky, thinking of my father and mother, and I began to cry. Everything is fantastic. Amigo Miller, adios, hasta Dios quiere (Good-bye, until God wants it). With a long life and much luck.

Mohammed Mrabet

Amigo Miller, forgive me. I was telling you stories and I forgot to tell you about France. Seven years ago Gallimard published my novel Love With a Few Hairs (L'Amour pour Quelques Cheveux) and the newspapers and magazines liked it very much. Then a Moroccan wrote about it in Le Monde, saying that probably Mohammed Mrabet did not exist, and that the book was by Paul Bowles even if there was such a person. Then Gallimard did not want to take any more of my books. When the

6

Moroccan newspapers saw <u>Le Monde</u>, they printed the article in Arabic and wrote their own insults after it. They said that anybody who couldn't write couldn't make a book. But I know the names of the men who wrote these articles, and they all have written books that they can't get published, so I understand why they are against me. Last year a small publisher called Le Dernier Terrain Vague published my book of stories called <u>M'Hashish</u>. My other books are not in French at all. And of course I have no Moroccan publisher, because there are none. So of course I'd like to have the name of a French publisher. Excuse me, Amigo Miller. I have two more things to say. The man in Utah who sent you my book <u>Look and Move On</u> says he is going to have an exhibit of your paintings, and he wants some of mine to show with them. I'm very happy about that, and I'm going to send him some. I'm waiting to hear how many he wants. The other thing is the photograph you said you would send. Thank you, even though I haven't seen it yet.

(Stroker 12, page 3)   Tangier, Morocco
                                          July 22nd, 1979

Irv Stettner/ Sroker magazine
New York, NY

Amigo Stettner:

        Thank you for your nice letter, and for the books you sent me at the same time. I was happy to have both letter and books. In your letter there were certain words on poverty. I found them when I read the letter carefully. It's not a question of poverty; a man's word is enough. We are all poor. When a man gives his word to another at a great distance --thousands of kilometers--and neither one knows the other, and one is an American and lives in New York, and the other is a Riffian living in Tangier, the one who gave his word must keep it. The Riffian is going to keep his word even before he gives it. The words I found in your letter made me both joyous and sad. And they made me think deeply, and I thought, and I remembered a story about something that happened here many years ago. Before I tell you the story, amigo, I have to say: Thanks to Henry Miller, and may Allah help him and give him long life. He's a man who wrote me one letter, and signed it Henry Miller, and I did not know who he was, and had never heard his name, because I don't read or write. And I took the letter to my friend Paul Bowles, the man who has translated all my books. When he took the letter in his hand, he exclaimed: What? Henry Miller? Then he read me the letter and explained it all to me. Afterward he spoke to me about Henry Miller, and showed me books of his. I was delighted, but I said to myself: How does it happen that such a fantastic man has written to me? And we went on writing to each other, and we are great friends, even though I've never seen him, because I have great respect for him. When I saw that his heart was as green as mine, the kind of heart that never dries up, either in summer or winter, then I knew that he was like me, and was my friend. A green heart lasts for many years, and the person with it lives for a long time. And I'll always go on writing to Henry Miller. I've seen reproductions of some of his paintings, and I think he sees the way I do, because his drawings look a little like mine, and I like them. Pues, amigo, the story is about a man's word. Because there are many millions of men in the world, and very few of them know the value of a man. Amigo, a Riffian from Tangier who used to travel around Morocco to buy things made in the south and sell them in the north, set out with fifteen other Riffians who worked for him, riding on camels and horses, for Marrakech. When he got there, he bought a great quantity of goods, all kinds of fantastic things that could be found only in Marrakech. The money he had with him was not enough to pay for everything. The Riffian began to ask around about some rich Marrakchi who might be willing to lend him the money. They showed him to a palace in the Medina, and the Riffian knocked on the door. The Marrakchi came out. Good Afternoon. Good Afternoon. I'm an importer from Tangier, and I have fifteen workers with me. The Marrakchi opened the door and invited all sixteen Riffians into his palace. They went and sat down. The Marrakchi ordered food to be prepared.

I need the loan of a hundred thousand dirhams, said the Riffian. And when you come to Tangier on business, I'll return it to you. Or if you don't come, I'll be back soon, and bring it to you. The Marrakchi said: Good. Then the sixteen Riffians spent three days in the Marrakchi's palace. The Marrakchi gave the hundred thousand dirhams to the Riffian, who took out a tiny box, saying to the Marrakchi: Keep this box carefully, until I repay the money. No, no. It's not necessary, said the Marrakchi. Yes, yes. Keep it for me, said the Riffian. And they said good-bye to the Marrakchi.

The Riffian went and paid for his goods, and the workers packed everything onto the animals, and they returned to Tangier.

Amigo, the word of a man, here it is. The Marrakchi looked at the box again and again for a week, saying to himself: What can be in such a tiny box that could be worth a hundred thousand dirhams? Finally, he could not wait, and he opened the box and looked inside. There was a piece of white cloth. He took it out and unfolded it. And there inside, my friend, the Marrakchi found one hair of the Riffian's beard. And the Marrakchi thought: If one hair of a man's beard is worth a hundred thousand dirhams, how much is the whole man going to be worth? And he said to himself: I must go to Tangier, even though I've got nothing to sell there. I want to see that Riffian. And he told himself it was not because he was afraid of losing his money. It's the man's word which is going to take me to Tangier, he said. And he went out and called to his servants, and they prepared everything for the journey, and set out over the plains for Tangier.

When the Marrakchi got to Tangier, he went straight to the Riffian's house. The Riffian greeted him and invited him and his servants inside. Amigo, the Riffians's entire family was running around getting dinner ready. They all spent a happy day, and when they finished eating at night, the Marrakchi brought out the tiny box. I didn't come here on account of my money. I came to ask you one question. Speak, said the Riffian. And the Marrakchi said: Tell me, if one hair of a man's beard costs a hundred thousand dirhams, what's the price of the man? The Riffian said: my friend, a man is priceless. And the Marrakchi asked the Riffian: And what is the price of a man's word? More than any treasure, the Riffian told him. The Marrakchi spent three days in the house, the Riffian gave him his hundred thousand dirhams, they embraced each other, and the Marrakchi went away. Good-bye, hasta Dios quiere (until God wants it).

Mohammed Mrabet

(Stroker 13, page 2)   Casa Zugari, Calle Ajdir,
                                           Merstakhoche, Tangier,
                                           Morocco   28/ix/79

My friend Stettner:

I greet you from Tangier, as if I was sitting talking with you. Thank you for sending the latest number of Stroker. Many Europeans enjoyed it, and so did I.

I'm writing this letter from the depths of my heart. This is the only way to write a letter to a friend. And I ask your forgiveness for the question I'm going to put to you.

As you may know, I can't leave this country, because the authorities won't grant me a passport. But in spite of that I want to arrange some exhibits of my drawings in the United States. The last one I had was at the Gotham Book Mart Gallery around 1975. If you know of a gallery that might like to do that, could you tell me? If you found one, could I send you the drawings, so you could take them there? Or is that impossible? If you haven't time, just tell me. I know people in New York are busy. As the ancients said: Even a push helps a man.

Friend Stettner, in the year 1953, I went one day to see a man who was ill. I took a girlfriend and a boy and his girlfriend with me. We sat eating dinner there, drinking wine, smoking kif. When I was half happy, the sick man came and went to sleep with his head on my thigh. And when my leg began to ache, I wanted to lift his head to put it somewhere else, but he was dead. Friend, good-bye, hasta Dios quiere, con mucha suerte (until God wants it, with much luck).

                                           Mohammed Mrabet

Tangier, Morocco
                                                               17/x/79

Dear Friend:

        Thank you for the good letter you sent me. I'm very happy with everything, and whatever letter I send you, if it interests you, you have my permission to print it in <u>Stroker</u>.

        I'm writing this letter now very m'hashish in my head. Also, and at the same time, I'm very happy. Happy because I'm recuperating now from my operation and feel like a lion. Amigo, I'm going to send you a small drawing of mine at the same time as this letter, and we'll see if you like it. I was pleased with everything you said in your letter. Because although I can't read English, Paul Bowles always reads my mail to me, I appreciated what you wrote. Amigo, I'm going to tell you a bit about a book I'm doing now. One day I went out with a friend in a rowboat into the Atlantic, to fish. We stopped rowing in order to cast our lines. It's a lot of work, fishing, and hopeless work. At the same time it's great for a man's health. When we had caught a few fish, we turned and started to go back towards the port. As we went along, I saw a small cage floating on top of the waves. When we got to it and I took it out of the water, I saw that it was new, and the only thing it had inside was a canary's head. This made me angry, nervous and sad all at the same time. If I had had a way of knowing whose canary it had been, and who was responsible for the thing, I could have beaten or even killed that person. Because I have twenty-two canaries in my house. I've lived twenty years with canaries. They're best early in the morning. You can hear thousands of different songs. And at the end of the afternoon on the terrace with many green plants and canaries, smoking pipes of kif, they make hundreds of different melodies. Querido Amigo Stettner, good-bye, hasta que Dios quiera. Much good luck and with much help from nobody. Only God can give and take away.

                                        Mohammed Mrabet

Tangier, Morocco
15/xi/79

Amigo Stettner:

Many thanks for the fine painting you sent me; I like it very much. It's an interesting picture to look at. I'm writing you this letter at eight o'clock in the evening, eating bread and cheese, drinking tea, and there's a strong wind outside, and now and then the rain comes down hard.

Amigo Stettner, I'm going to send you a piece of my new book soon, and we'll see if you like it. In it you'll see that I was in the hospital for twenty-one days before I was let out one day at ten thirty in the morning, that I went home and found such destruction that I fell ill again, and was back in the hospital at two the same day, in the same bed, feeling worse than ever.

Amigo Stettner, everything is good. Everything that happens to a man during his life, bad or good, he must make good by giving thanks for being alive. I always say everything is good. Amigo Stettner, I'll send you more drawings if you need them for your magazine. I'm happy to have your drawing. I'll make a good frame for it myself. It came yesterday in the afternoon, and I brought it to show Paul. He liked it. When I went home I took out five or six frames I have, and there was one that will fit it perfectly. I placed the drawing beside a low light and sat down, very high. I saw that the two people in the drawing loved each other very much.

Amigo Stettner, we know that a man has no price.
Adios, hasta Dios quiere,
With good luck and the help of God.

Mohammed Mrabet

Merstakhoche
Tangier, Morocco
5/xii/79

Amigo Stettner:

       I am going to speak to you seriously. First, to thank you for the two extra copies of Stroker, and for your letter, which had in it something I didn't know. Your letter makes me speak. Just one word in your letter gave me the desire to write to you. As you said, a man has no price. You are right in that, but then there are few men. What is this man who told a French girl he had translated my work? Amigo Stettner, I shall speak, and you must not be angry with me. At the moment I am m'hashish in my head, and the report of such a person who lies to girls in such a way disgusts me. I don't know such a character, friend. I never even saw him in a box of sardines. Amigo Stettner, I'm not lying to you. The only man who has made all my translations is Paul Bowles. And there is a fantastic woman who translated my book M'Hashish from English into French. Her name is Claude Thomas. And Carlos Lacerda in Rio de Janeiro translated The Lemon from English into Portuguese. (Now he's dead.) An Italian also translated M'Hashish into his language. But they all used the English version. And I have a friend here in Tangier named Mohamed Choukri, who has never been to America, who translated a story of mine into Arabic from Moghrebi. Amigo Stettner, as the ancients said: When you can't reach the pear on a high branch, you decide it's not a good one. And one bad fish ruins the entire barrel. There's nobody in New York who has made translations of my work, nor in all of America. And the one who says he has done that is a wretched man. Or perhaps he dreamed of doing it, and now he believes in his dream. Amigo Stettner, many times when I'm high I bathe all night in the Atlantic. And when I open my eyes I find myself in bed. But that doesn't make me think the dream was true. And that kind of person might be drugged day and night..who knows? Forgive me, amigo Stettner. I'd like to know that girl. Please give her many salutations from my heart. I'm here, and can't see anyone, like a fish in the swimming pool. Only in the summer do a few friends come to visit me. Amigo Stettner, I'm going now to tell you a poem that I learned when I was shut into the black room. There are three people in the poem: two men and a girl. The one who has the girl, why don't you let me have her? Only to spend tonight with me, and in the morning you can take her back.

I dress well and take good care of myself. My darling, I'm suffering from everything that God sends. The one who has her, the lithe one, disturbs me. My breast above your breast, my loved one, your hair loose and flowing. Coming up from the market, I carry with me a ring, and it is worth the price of two boats. My loved one, they went away on a voyage. Amigo Stettner, I'm writing this letter, and if there is an error in it I ask your forgiveness. And that poem, I learned it when I was fifteen years old. Many years ago. It was taught me by some friends. We spent all day and night in the black room, but at least there we could smoke and eat hash. We were five, and each one invented something. And amigo Stettner, we stayed in that room for one year and eight months. The next letter I'll send you will have another poem we made up there, longer than this one. And these poems are about events that really happened. Because we know very well that many men have died because of women, and also that wars have started on account of one woman, wars in which thousands of men have died. And many of the young men in the black room were there because of girls. Amigo Stettner, sometimes in the street you see a bitch, and behind her there are ten dogs fighting. And all the dogs are of one quarter of the town. Then another dog from another part of town comes up and takes the bitch away without any trouble, and leaves the ten looking after them, and not one of them dares to follow them. Amigo Stettner, adios, hasta Dios quiere. Much luck. The drawing I sent you is meant for you. A long life and perfect health,

Mohammed Mrabet

Tangier, Morocco
7/xii/79

Dear Friend Stettner:

       Today is Friday, and it's seven o'clock in the evening, and very dark outside. This letter will come out of a deep cave in my heart. I shall make you a little sad, because I'm sad myself. I feel very ill and depressed. Because life is boring sometimes. Amigo Stettner, I'm married, I have three children, and my wife lives by herself with her mother, and I live alone. I have to pay all the food and expenses of the children and the woman, and suffer as a result. There is no one to change the law, no way to earn a living here, no way to be happy. You know well, amigo, that Paul isn't young, and can't translate books faster. I have many tapes full of stories and novels that a younger man could translate fast. Where is such a young man? Amigo Stettner, I'm going to give you a poem about my life. In the year 1954 in the black room.

I knocked very hard on the door
And a great beauty came out
Black eyes and a criminal face
She invited me into her sala
And made me sit down on a throne
Then she took out a sebsi and filled it
And gave it to me, and I smoked
And she filled it again and again
And then we went into the chamber
Dance! Dance, Lolo!
And when your lover comes
We'll give him a feast
Dance! Dance, my girl
Give me a kiss with those lips,
Before I disappear
Maria, the informer,
Told everything to the police
They snapped the handcuffs on me
And carried me to the Mendoubia
Each Judge passes down a sentence
And they gave me twelve years
Mother, pray for me

They put me aboard a ship
And carried me to Melilla
They sat me down on a mat
And gave me glasses of tea and cakes
And porridge of brown beans
And Riffian custard
I'll never forget you,
My beloved Maria

Amigo Stettner, I've never put any of these poems into any of my books. As we say here: If a son is born to you, throw him into the thornbushes. Then he'll be a man. And if you care for him the way you care for a girl, always giving him the best of everything, you can be sure you won't end up having a man in the house. If you have a daughter in your house whose name is Anne, you'll have a son whose name is Maria. That's true, Amigo Stettner. If a man doesn't suffer, he can't know what life is about. And if a man hasn't mixed with every kind of human being, including the worst, so he can know the best and the worst, he can never be sure whether he's a man or not. Because, Amigo Stettner, there are men like me who have slept in cafés on the floor, eaten badly, gone badly dressed, and suffered in all kinds of ways, and yet they're still alive, in good health, able to work and able to live well. Amigo Stettner, I'm going to send you a photograph. It was taken at the beach café. (My next book is called The Beach Café.) Adios, hasta Dios quiere. With a long life and good luck. And a man has no price.

Mohammed Mrabet

Tangier, Morocco
                                        22/xii/79

Amigo Stettner:

          Many good thoughts and salutations. Yesterday the
twenty-first of December something strange happened. And when it
happened I thought of you, Amigo Stettner. So I'm writing you on the
twenty-second. What happened? All fantastic. Some friends of mine had
bought a fine sheep, a sheep of a year and a half, and we were all in a café.
We joined together, seven of us, to buy the sheep. And we killed it there at
the café, and one of my friends said to me: Will you bring my share of the
meat to my house later? I've got work to do now. And I said I would. We
cut the meat up among seven men, and I took two shares of it and put
them both into my car. Then I went to see Paul, and we talked a bit about
my work. What with the stuff I smoke, I forgot about the meat until it was
half past ten in the evening. I saw the big packet in the car, and thought:
Well, my friend will have eaten something else by now, but I'll drop the
mutton off at his house anyway. I knocked on the door. Nothing. The
lights were all on, the television was playing loud. A neighbor told me that
they had been up on the terrace a while ago making a fire in a big mijmah,
and had taken it down to get some heat, because it was a very cold night.
When I heard that, I backed up, put my head down, and went running at
the door like a bull, and suddenly both the door and I were inside the
house. And my friend and his children and all his family were lying on the
floor unconscious. First I opened all the doors and windows, then I put the
big mijmah outside. Then I threw water on the faces of all the people. The
neighbor arrived, and found me rubbing onions over the faces of the
family. Nothing serious happened, fortunately. Afterwards the neighbor
and I put the door back onto its hinges. Then he went away and I stayed
with my friend. I went to the kitchen and cut up both pieces of meat into
cubes, and made shish-kebab with it. By then it was one in the morning.
His wife began to feel better, and she got up and made some tea while I
grilled the meat over the coals. Everyone ate and drank tea. Then I said:
I'm going to tell you good-night. My friend looked at me and said:
Mrabet, this is the third time you've saved my life. The first time, before I
was married, you pulled me out of the ocean. The second time you saved
me from two men and two women. The ones who had knives, all of them,
and wanted to cut me up. And now you've saved me and my wife and my

children and all the rest of the family. I said: I didn't do anything, my friend. It's only that the world isn't tired of you yet. Amigo Stettner, adios, hasta Dios quiere. A man has no price.

Mohammed Mrabet

Tangier, Morocco
                                                23/xii/79

Querido Amigo Stettner:

   Your letter arrived at Calle Ajdir at half past four in the afternoon, yesterday. That was Saturday and this is Sunday. I liked your letter, amigo Stettner. It made me sad because you said parts of my letter depressed you. I think you are right, though, since, amigo Stettner, anyone who has a good heart and can understand what words mean, can be made sad by a letter. Amigo Stettner, when a man starts out to write a letter he may have only one thing in his mind, but as he writes he finds many other things to say, things that he didn't know were in his mind.

   Amigo Stettner, I'm not a writer. I've never been a writer because I can't read or write. But ever since I was little I've been with fantastic people and seen fantastic things. My real work is fishing, and sometimes I buy and sell things. I have a little house beside the ocean. There I work a lot. There is no sound of automobiles; there is only the sea. I'm very happy to be living in this country, and I swear to you, Amigo Stettner, as Moslems swear, by Allah, if you should come to Tangier and I were to show you corners of Morocco, you would agree with me that it's a paradise. Paul came here almost fifty years ago, and he has always liked it, and he has always liked Tangier. A song says: Tangier is a bride, the bride of the Chemel (the east). She is tall and her trees are tall. Why, amigo Stettner? If you go only three miles out of town you find forests. And even if you're poor, you can live. If you're rich, you live better than anywhere else. In the cafés everyone is happy. Wherever you go, people are laughing. The only ones who criticize are the ones who hate to work. They want to earn money without working. Amigo Stettner, if you think you're going to fall in love with the French girl, remember that I'm already in love with her. I send many greetings to her, and I wish her much good luck. Amigo Stettner, I'm going to give you the words they sing while I'm dancing for the Jilala.

   Ah, my love! Ah, my love! This hour is mine. Listen, then to me. I stand here, and you must be by my side. Ah, my love! Ah, my love, help me! Allah! Allah! May they bring it to me, that I may have it. And still he has not come. Call to him! You must call to him! Sidi Baghdad is Moulay Abdelqader. Ah, my love, hand me steel, tempered, sharp. I slash my flesh, the blood comes out. The blood starts to flow. Ah, my love! Ah, my love! He has come. He stands by my side.

He touches me, and I feel something I cannot say. Ah, my love! Moulay Abdelqader el Jilali! Allah! Allah who is my God, thanks be to Him! Thanks be to Him, ya Allah! My loved one has heard my voice and is by my side, he who brings me help and who blesses everything that is mine. He is by my side. That which is newly sharpened is in my hand and the blood is flowing. Ah, my love! Ah, my love, may Allah be with me and with you! You are beside me, the knife is in my hand, and the blood wells from my arm. I weep and I tell everything I know to you, my love. Be with me and the others here. All of me is yours, ah, my love!

* * " * * " * * " * * " * * " * * " * * " * * " * * " * *

Good bye, hasta Dios quiere, much good luck
and a long life. With the help of God, and
<u>El hombre no tiene precio.</u>

M. Mrabet

Casa Zugari, Calle Ajdir,
Merstakhoche,
Tangier, Morocco
14/i/80

Dear Friend Stettner:

Many greetings and hugs. (Grandes abrazos) I'm very happy with your two letters, and I like the photograph a lot. And I want to send many thanks for the check you enclosed in your last letter. Amigo Stettner, you know I don't write to you in order to earn money. I write to you out of a feeling of great friendship. We are friends. But I do appreciate what you sent, and I thank you. I'm happy.

I had terrible difficulty getting your letter out of the post office. All my papers are now made out in a new name the government recently gave me, so that I'm no longer allowed to call myself Mrabet. The new name the government has given me, and which is on all my documents is Mohammed ben Chaib el Hajjam. And now Mrabet exists only in my books. There at the post-office great insults were exchanged, Amigo Stettner. One young man who works there with his pen, sitting at a desk, asked me for my Carte Nationale when I presented my paper. "How does it happen that the letter says Mrabet and your card says el Hajjam? You think you can steal that way?" I said: "Shame on you for insulting me like this!" "I'm telling you. And don't you stir from here. I'm calling the police," he told me. And I said: "Call them if you want, and then call the fire brigade, and then you'd better call an ambulance. Because the police won't take me away from here until I've put you into the ambulance." Everybody in the post-office stopped what he was doing. The place was full of both Moroccans and Europeans. I swear to you, Amigo Stettner, I took off my selham and laid it on a table and said to the young man: "Do you know who you are?" "Who am I?" he asked me. "Don't you know me? Don't you remember me?" "Who are you?" he wanted to know. "I'm the man who always screwed your mother. I'm the man who bought your clothes for you. How many times when you were still in school did you come to my mahal and stay with me? How many schoolbooks and pens and notebooks have I bought for you? And now you've got a job here. The only men who treat their friends like this are the ones who sell themselves for money." Then I heard a man speaking to me. I heard: "Senor Mrabet". I turned around and saw a friend of mine. "Ah, Sidi Mjidou!" "What is the matter, Mrabet?" he said. "Oh, I'm with this son of fountain pens and bed," I told him. "He tells me I've come to steal here." Finally they did give me the letter. I took it and went out of the post office, laughing to myself. We're living in the world of pens and beds now, Amigo Stettner, and we have no way of knowing which ones are the sons of their fathers. Why can't we know? Thousands and thousands of sons of whores exist, and they don't know who their fathers are. Amigo Stettner, I'm making a small restaurant later in the spring. It's right on the ocean. If you ever think of coming to Tangier, you have my address, or you can send me a letter so I'll know which day you're arriving, and can meet you either at the port or the airport. If you like my house, you can stay in it for as long as you like. And if you prefer to be beside the sea, I have two fantastic rooms over the sand, and it's there I'm going to make my little restaurant when warm weather comes. I received a letter from the Qadi saying I'll have to pay a fantastic amount of money to my wife. You know we live apart. They're sucking my blood. So naturally I must make the restaurant, because I know I can earn money with it. I have to pay nine dollars a day for the children. It doesn't matter. If you have health, you have everything. Amigo Stettner, I'm not going to forgive you if you come to Morocco without coming to visit me. It would give me great pleasure to see you. Adios. Hasta Dios quiere, with much luck and a long life.

                                        Mohammed Mrabet

28

Merstakhoche
                                                    Tangier, Morocco
                                                    22/i/80

Querido Amigo Stettner:

          Here I am again. Thank you for your good letter, the most recent one. I found it very interesting, and it made a deep impression on me. I like to see that there are men who can earn their living the way you have. Not like the young men that come in cans, or the ones that come wrapped in plastic, the way they come nowadays. Not like the young men who live in bed. They get up at three, in the afternoon, spend an hour and a half in the bathroom and another hour and a half in front of the mirror and another hour to get to the door so they can go out. They don't count as men, or even as women. Amigo Stettner, I'm going to tell you a bit about my second novel THE LEMON. I think you said you'd read it. One night I had nowhere to sleep. There was nowhere I could go. I walked along and came to a big tree, and I sat down under it. Then I went to sleep, and while I slept it began to rain. When I felt the rain wetting me, I was afraid to turn over for fear the other side of me would get wet too. Amigo Stettner, and there's another part of my life that isn't in THE LEMON, when I used to go out along the beach to the Monopolio and help the fishermen pull in the nets. Whenever they pulled fish out of the water they gave me my share. And I always earned enough to get by. I was ten or eleven then. Amigo Stettner, afterwards I lived only by buying and selling fish. Then I worked with a pick and shovel. Amigo Stettner, I also worked in people's houses unblocking their toilets. When I was fifteen I started to work for the first time in a bar of whores. I sat in a chair by the door, and whoever wanted to make trouble or didn't feel like paying for his drinks, or tried to take a girl by force, got his face turned around backward. It didn't matter who he was, Tarzan or Hercules. After that, Amigo Stettner, I made hundreds of enemies here in Tangier, so I left that kind of work, and began to buy a kilo of kif and prepare it myself as it should be prepared. I sold a big box of it for five pesatas, and managed to live on the profits. And Amigo Stettner, I'll tell you something I've never told anybody. One afternoon I was standing on some rocks watching the fish at the bottom of very clear water. I had a friend with me, and he didn't know how to swim. In my hand I had a grenade. My friend could not help me in the water, so I had to

29

do it all by myself. I saw a place where there was a good quantity of fish and threw the grenade into the water. I had a long line, about twenty meters long, with a very sharp stick attached to the end of it. At the other end of the line I had a glass sphere floating. As I caught the fish I would spear their necks with the stick and threaded them onto the line. I took off my clothes and jumped into the water with the equipment. I caught sixty kilos of fish. If the gendarmes had caught me I'd have got twenty years. When I got back to the beach with all the fish slung over my shoulder, I began to pile them into big baskets I had brought along. A French woman with a small black dog came by and watched. Did you catch all those fish? she asked me. I said yes, I had. How did you do it? she wanted to know. With a net, I told her. Too bad I haven't got a cook, she said. And I said: Madame, you can pick out any fish you want here, and I'll cook it for you. Ah, she said, but who's going to eat it with me? I said I'd eat it with her. She looked at me and said: I'd be delighted. I asked her if she had a car, and she said she did. Well, from here we'll take my fish down to the market and leave my friend there to sell it. Then I'll go home and change my clothes, and go back to your house. She said: Why don't we do something else? Why don't we go straight to the market and leave your friend there, and then you come back to my house? I said that was fine. I packed all the fish into the boot of her car and we drove to the market where I left all the fish except one big loup de mer. I got back into the car with her and her dog, and we went to her house. Amigo Stettner, you must forgive me if I don't tell you the whole story. I think I told you enough. I can say that I stayed with her six months. Of course many people were laughing at me and making jokes about me. I didn't enjoy that life even though it was good. I went back to my fish. Amigo Stettner, I'm waiting for you in Tangier. If you want to come, my house is your house. You know that I can't leave this country. If I could, I assure you I'd come and see you. Adios. Hasta Dios quiere, with the help of Allah. And a long life.

Mohammed Mrabet

30

Tangier, Morocco
                                              1/iii/80

Amigo Stettner:

      I'm happy with the magazine, which arrived. And excuse me for waiting so long to write you. I had a lot of work to do. I'm making a novel and I'm almost finished recording it. The title is Qaftan. Amigo Stettner, I wanted to send you something else, but when I thought just now of Qaftan, I decided to tell you a bit of that instead. And I'll leave the other story for another letter. Amigo Stettner, this is about a young farmer who went far from his tchar, like fifty kilometers, and began to live all by himself in the mountains. He built a big house, using only trees, and many smaller ones to put animals into, in the same manner. And he planted a large orchard.

      After several years the young man went back to his tchar and got married. Then, taking the animals he needed from his family's sheds, he started back to the forest with his bride. Amigo Stettner, the first year he had to be the midwife for her baby girl. Both the mother and child were healthy. When the girl was three years old, she tried to play with the goats. They butted her with their horns. If she tried to play with the dogs, they bit her. When she went to play with the cows, they kicked her. If she played with the hens, they pecked at her legs. Amigo Stettner, there was nobody else living there in the wilderness. The nearest child was fifty kilometers away. Her mother could not have any more children. That child was only an accident.

      One morning, Amigo Stettner, her mother took her with her down to a big spring below the house to fetch some water. The child got to the spring first, because she skipped ahead. When she looked into the water, she saw her reflection there, and it moved just the same as she did. She called to her mother: Yimma! Yimma! There's a girl here like me. Ah, yes, Souad, she said. And Souad said: Yimma! She moves her hands and her head. Does she live there, Yimma? Yes, Souad, said her mother. Then I'm always going to come here, Yimma, said Souad. Very good, said her mother.

      Amigo Stettner, I'm going to make a jump. The girl would spend all day, from the time the sun came up until it went down, talking to her friend in the water. After a while some other farmers arrived in the region and built some houses there. Finally there were about twenty houses, with a few women, a few men, and many children and animals.

Then there were more vegetables and fruit than they needed. Souad's father, when he saw that his daughter was obsessed by the reflection, built a big well near the house. And when it was full of water Souad, who now was nine or ten years old, and very pretty, would go to the well and see herself in the water. But now, instead of seeing herself in an exact reflection, she saw her friend down there dressed in a fantastic qaftan. Her mother and father did everything they could to make her go and play with the other children, but she hated all of them, and all the animals as well. She would see her friend wearing the splendid qaftan, and talk with her, and now the friend in the water answered her, so that Souad was even happier.

Amigo Stettner, you mustn't be annoyed if I keep leaving out big parts of the story. One evening Souad and her parents were eating their supper. The man turned to his wife and said: There's a woman here who teaches girls how to sew. Why don't we take Souad to her? Then Souad, hearing this, said: And what am I going to do there? Why, you'll learn how to make clothes that people can wear, her mother told her. Good, said Souad. And she began to go to the woman to learn how to sew. She sat beside her and the woman showed her everything. There were other girls present, but the woman gave Souad private lessons. She stayed for three years with the woman.

In her house Souad had her own room, and she could bolt the door. Amigo Stettner, when she went to sleep each night, soon after she shut her eyes, the friend would appear in the room. She would say: Good evening, Souad, here I am, talking to you. Souad could not answer; she could only look at the qaftan her friend was wearing. Amigo Stettner, Souad is going to begin working on that qaftan. And for thirty-seven years she will work on it. And she's going to finish it. Amigo Stettner, I write you this piece of a story, and soon I'll send you a part of my youth, spent in Spain. Adios, hasta Dios quiere, with much good luck,

Mohammed Mrabet

P.S.--Amigo Stettner, forgive me. I've noticed that now, in the year of 1980, men do have a price. And the price is one dollar. It's too bad.

32

Casa Zugari, Calle Ajdir,
Merstakhoche, Tangier,
Morocco.
30/iii/80

Amigo Stettner:

Thank you for your letters and the copies of <u>Stroker</u> you sent. I give those extra copies to Europeans and Americans. Recently a group of American students who were here went away with two. And a woman from Denmark took three: one for her, one for her father, and one for her mother. A terrible Spaniard came through Tangier last week, a man I detest, (and some day I'm going to deprive him of his neck) took another copy. Amigo Stettner, this letter I'm writing you now, I don't know how it's going to come out, and if something awful happens in the middle of it, you mustn't hold it against me. Because I don't know where I am, I don't know what I'm doing, I'm very bad and very sad, really crying..I don't know how it will finish. The twenty-fifth of March was my birthday, forty years. I was in my house with a group of Jilala, playing and singing. Some American girls were there, part of an exchange group. There were about twenty guests. I was in the kitchen; I made a big dinner, and a great many pastries and cakes, and I did it all myself, with no help from anybody. Everyone was happy, the music was strong, people were dancing. Amigo Stettner, I heard someone knocking on the door. When I opened it, there was my brother, the youngest one. I saw that he was crying. What's wrong? He said: Twenty minutes ago our grandmother died. Don't be sad on her account, because she lived through more than a hundred years, and died healthy. From the day she was born she never saw a doctor. I told him: Yes. Well, I'll be there later. Amigo Stettner, I served everyone, everyone ate, I made tea and brought in the cakes and pastries. Everyone was eating and speaking. I said nothing to anyone, and went on as if nothing at all had happened. The musicians went on playing. Finally everyone went home. Amigo Stettner, I loved my grandmother because she loved me. When I would go to visit my mother, she would be there. I would greet her and sit down beside her, and she would talk to me, and explain all sorts of things to me. I could see that the words were not coming out of her mouth, but out of her heart, and the words were jewels. Losing her was losing a great fortune. And today, Amigo Stettner, the thirtieth of March, I went out of the house in the morning, to go to the flea-market, where I bought a few little things. Then I took them somewhere else and sold them. That's how I earn a living these days. Amigo Stettner, all this is too much to bear. Something happened to my youngest son this morning; I don't know what because I wasn't there. I was trying to earn some money. Two legs are broken, Amigo Stettner. You know I don't live with my wife, and haven't for two years. I always have to pay for her. Even though that happened to the child, no one came to say a word to me. When I was in the market buying the food for the children, a friend asked me: How's the little boy? I said: What little boy? Your son Ahmed, he said. Why? Has something happened? Don't you know anything about it? he cried. At ten o'clock in the morning he got his legs broken. That was all he knew. Nobody had told him what had happened, or how. Just that Ahmed had two broken legs. That's the fault of his mother, who took him away from me so I could never see him. Amigo Stettner, this letter made me give you a part of my new book, which I haven't finished because I have to put more into it. It's called Married with Papers. Amigo Stettner, first piece: my wife said: I want to make a trip through Morocco. Yes, I said, I'd like it, too. It's too bad there's no money. She suggested I borrow it. I told her: Nobody's going to lend me enough to make the kind of trip you want. Then she said: And what about the books and the drawings you make? I'm not Picasso, I told her. And I'm not Tennessee Williams, either. I'm a man who doesn't eat unless he works, and you know it. When I go to market you're always sad. And when I give you money to go to market you're always happy. Because no matter how much I give you, you always come back without a guirch in you bag. If you did what real women do, you'd save some money every day to put toward the trip, instead of buying three times as much food as we can eat, and throwing it all into the garbage pail every night. When I said that to her, she stared at me and said: Are you going to eat? I said: Yes, I'd like to. She gave me my dinner, and I ate it. Afterward I worked for several hours, and when I got into bed to sleep, I couldn't sleep. In the morning I thought I was dying. Three days I was in bed, and she didn't want anyone to know, so she said nothing. Until a friend happened to come by and see me, and went and spread the news. My friends took me to the hospital. Alone in a room with the door shut, and a tube stuck into each arm to feed me. That's the way I was when my beloved wife came to visit me. She came in and shut the door. Then she stood looking at me. Amigo Stettner, the first words I heard were: You're alive. I stayed twenty-one days in the hospital, Amigo Stettner. I got out at ten in the morning on the twenty-first day. I got to my house and opened the door. In the hall I saw that all of my plants had been uprooted from their pots and were lying in piles of dirt on the floor. My canaries had been stamped to death inside their cages. The bathtub was full of water, and in the water were all my cassettes of stories and parts of novels, together with the tape-recorder at the bottom of the tub. And all my clothes were soaking in a laundry tub with six or seven quarts of chlorox poured on top. I went out onto the terrace and suddenly began to vomit, and that gave me pains in my stomach. At two o'clock that afternoon I was back in the same bed in the same room in the same hospital. Amigo Stettner, I'm going to write to you tomorrow again. I have a story which I think will interest you. That señora who calls herself Barbara, I'm delighted to know her from far away. My doors and windows are open day and night. The day when she wants to come, I hope you can let me know in advance so that I can meet her at the airport or at the maritime port. I'd be happy to meet her. Because as you know I can't go anywhere. My exhibit of drawings is on now at the Gotham Book Mart, thanks to you, and I can't be there to see it. Dear friend Stettner, I'm sad about Henry Miller's health. Many greetings to him, and wish him a long life. There are many others who are even sadder than I to hear that he is ill, I'm certain, for thousands of people love him. Adios, hasta Dios guiere. Much light and much power.

Mohammed Mrabet

Merstakhoche, Tangier,
                                                Morocco.
                                                2/iv/80

Querido amigo Stettner:

      When I give you my word about something, I must keep it. I'm not going to speak much about myself. I swear, friend, these last days I don't know what I'm doing. Like someone who has drunk two bottles of vodka. You know what happens to such people. I'm lost. The past two nights I haven't slept. I smoke three rebtas a day. It's a great deal. When I get into bed, hour after hour I lie there thinking. Sometimes I'm the richest man in the world. Sometimes I'm a prince. Sometimes I'm the poorest wretch who exists. Sometimes I begin to weep in my bed. Very nervous. Everyone else is asleep. I'm sitting in the darkness, with only the light from the sky that comes in through the windows. I'm sitting with everything beside me, so I can brew coffee if I want. I'm very fond of Nescafé. I must drink a litre and a half or even two litres of it each day. If I don't happen to take it in the morning when I get up, I feel that I've missed something. And I go on smoking cigarette after cigarette. The darkness goes, and day arrives. Amigo Stettner, I'm not inventing, I'm writing you this letter from the depth of the veins of my heart. Very sad. I feel horrible. It doesn't matter. We have to accept everything that happens to us in our life. Because when we are born, it is a result of our desire to be born. Those who have none are not born alive. Whatever happens during the life of a man, good or bad, has to be accepted, and with thanks to Allah.

      Amigo Stettner, that's all I want to say about myself. I don't want to go on. I'd like to give you a very old story, one which I like, because I appreciate real people. There was a man named Abdelqader. He was extremely religious, and he had a black man working for him. What work did he perform? He heated a little water early in the morning, so Abdelqader could wash when he got up. And wherever Abdelqader went, he would say to the black man: My son, you must be at my side. Abdelqader wore an ancient, ragged djellaba, and his servant, whom he called his son, was always dressed in white and green silk. The people in the street would call to the black, and speak against Abdelqader. The black would answer: No one in the world can say anything against this great saint. The people would say: A great saint? Yes! he would cry. One day when they were talking this way, the black said: Two days from now the pacha of the city is going to burn a black like me, because he hit a white man. The white man was his master, and he wouldn't pay him. And the saint is going to save him. I've seen the saint riding on a lion, and I've seen him turn himself into a white bird and fly away, and many other strange things. So now, good-bye.

Amigo Stettner, two days later the soldiers took the black out of the dungeon. He was a wonderful young man, tall and healthy. They tied his arms behind him to a big pole, and piled tons of wood underneath and around him. But Abdelqader arrived and took off his old djellaba, and put it around the shoulders of the prisoner. They lighted the fire. The young man's father and mother and family were watching and weeping. That fire was not one for burning one man; it was for burning an entire city. The black who worked for Abdelqader went over to the young man's family and said: Don't cry. You can go home at rest in your minds, and in a little while your son will join you.

Yes, amigo Stettner. When all the wood had burned, the djellaba that covered the young man was still the same, and the young man had no burns on him. The soldiers had gone away, sure that he was dead. Abdelqader went over to him, and took him away from the post, removed the djellaba, and accompanied him home. The family was overjoyed. Amigo Stettner, one day Moulay Abdelqader was walking in the street with his old djellaba, when he came to a large mansion where many notables were going in through the door. He thought he would go in and see what was happening in the courtyard. But the guards would not let him in. Why? Because of his ragged djellaba. Abdelqader went home, and changed his clothes, putting on the finest robes of silk. Then he returned to the same house. Amigo Stettner, this time when he came to the door they bowed in front of him, and welcomed him. They invited him into the banquet room and gave him a seat among the most important men. Soon the meal was brought in. They began to eat, all from the same enormous dish in the center of the taifor. And they ate with their hands and put the food into their mouths. But Abdelqader pushed all the food he took into the sleeves of his robes. The gravy ran down his arms. The others stared at him. What are you doing? they asked him. You're soiling your clothes. Yes, he said. When they bowed so low in front of me, they weren't bowing to me at all.

What were they bowing to, then? they asked him.

38

They were bowing to silk, he said. Silk was welcome. So, he said, putting his arms into the food up to his elbows and moving them around in the mess, so silk has got to eat!

Amigo Stettner, Abdelqader got up from the taifor and said: When I came looking poor, they drove me away from the door. And when silk arrived dancing and singing, it got in easily. And with great respect on all sides. So they found a good seat for the silk, with the sages and the important and intelligent people. Please forgive me. And he went out, and everyone was shocked and cold. Each one felt a sort of fear. Abdelqader arrived at his house, went in, and found the black waiting. What? Are you still up? he asked him. Master, said the black man, I knew you weren't going to eat at that house, and I've been waiting for you to come back so we could eat dinner together. And Abdelqader remained looking at him, and he sat down, and they ate together.

My son, Abdelqader said. Now you're seventeen years old, and I'm an old man. You must get married. I'm going to ask the pacha to give me his daughter for you. How can that ever be? the black said. You think the pacha is going let me marry his daughter? Abdelqader said: Don't speak that way. What is black skin? Tomorrow I'm going to see the pacha. The next day they went together to the pacha's palace. When the pacha saw Abdelqader, he opened his doors and said: Come in. They sat down in a room, and Abdelqader told the pacha why he had come. But for whom do you want her? the pacha asked him. For my son here, said Abdelqader. What, Moulay Abdelqader? You've come to insult me? My white daughter with your black son?

Abdelqader said: My black son is worth more than your white daughter. Then the pacha told him: Don't be hasty. I'll ask my daughter. The pacha went and asked his daughter, and she said: Yes, baba, I'd like to marry him. When he came back to the room, there was no sign of either Abdelqader or his son. Where can they be? he asked his daughter. They flew out the window, she said. Adios, hasta Dios quiere, con mucha suerte, and soon I'll write you again.

Mohammed Mrabet

39

(*Stroker 16*, page 35)   Merstakhoche, Tangier,
                                           Morocco.
                                           8/iv/80

Amigo Stettner:

          Many greetings and salutations. The first thing I'm
going to write is a story I want to tell you. A magic story. Amigo Stettner,
in the year 1978, early one morning I went to the ocean to fish. I got to the
edge of the water. The waves were hitting the rocks very bad. I began to
fish with a volantin, which I would throw out into the water. And the
waves hit the cliffs and made clouds of spray that left colors in the water.
Violet with red and green. And inside the colors I saw the face of a
beautiful girl. That was all I could see of her---only her face, smiling at me
from the water. And I stood there looking at her. A woman in the water? I
said to myself. And the waves came and washed her against the rocks with
great force. I stood looking for a long time. Then she disappeared. I could
no longer see any face in the water. I went on fishing, and they began to
come faster and faster: pageot, loup de mer, and other kinds. I caught a
great many fish. Then I saw that the sun was overhead, and I decided to go
to the forest and rest until it got cool, when I would go home, back to the
city. I sat in a shady part of the forest, ate some lunch, and lay back to rest
a bit. Of course I fell asleep. And I seemed at one point to hear a woman
screaming. I woke up, startled by the sound in the silence of the forest. It
was already getting dark, and the jackals were howling. I got up and
climbed up to the trail and sat down facing the forest, and lit a pipe of kif.
As I sat watching the forest grow dark, I suddenly saw something filmy
and brilliant red floating among the branches. It swayed from side to side,
and came nearer. Then I saw that it was a woman. I jumped up, and she
alighted on the ground and stood still, about ten feet away. She looked at
me and smiled. I stared at her, and realized that it was the same face I had
seen in the water. Then she began to float upwards and backwards,
moving her arms slowly in the air. I watched her disappear into the
blackness of the forest. I picked up my things. At half past eight I was in
the city. I sold my fish to a wholesaler, and went home. I washed, ate
something, and made a pot of tea. Then as I drank the tea I began to smoke
kif, and made four drawings. I got up and went to bed. When I was asleep,
I saw that the same woman had somehow got into my house, and was in
the room with me, stark naked. A fantastic body. A face you can't
describe. Black hair that shown more than gold. In her hand she held a

braided leather whip, and she came to me and pulled off the sheet, and ripped my pyjamas off my body, and began to beat me. And I was yelling, and could do nothing to stop her. Suddenly I heard a loud knocking at the door. I opened my eyes and saw that I was naked and lying on the floor. The teapot and the tray and glasses were upset. I put on my pyjama bottoms and went to answer the knocking. The man who lives downstairs under me was standing there. What's the matter, Mrabet? Come in, I told him. Then I explained everything to him. It was your fault, he told me. When you first saw her in the ocean, why did you stay so long looking at her? She may have many friends like you. Then he went back downstairs. I made some coffee. It was four o'clock in the morning. I drank the coffee, took my things, and set out for the ocean. Amigo Stettner, as soon as I started to fish, there she was in the water. No fisherman could catch as many fish as I caught that day and every day afterward. She was always there helping me. Another night she came to my house when I was asleep and gave me another terrible beating, and again there was banging on the door, and I put on my pyjama pants, and opened the door. It was the same neighbor. Again? he said. Again, I told him. But Mrabet, he said, your body is covered with welts. I looked into the mirror and saw that it was true. My neighbor said: Are you crying, Mrabet? Who would have believed it? And only in one eye. Your right eye is crying all by itself. Yes, I said. I've seen my eye weeping, and I can't believe it myself.

The next morning, amigo Stettner, I didn't go fishing. I went to the market with two friends of mine and bought all kinds of food, so we could spend the night fishing. And it happened that way. That night we all went out to the ocean to fish. There we were, fishing in the dark, and the only one to catch any was I. And each time I caught one I had to call to the other two for help, because they were so heavy. I caught seven merones. Finally I lay down and napped between the rocks. The girl arrived this time dressed in her red gown, and she was very friendly. Amigo Stettner, it was this way: if I slept at home in my bed, she was going to come and beat me. But if I slept near the water, she would be my friend. A friend of mine had a cave not far from that part of the coast. It was a large cave and he lived all the time in it. I took my things there and began to live with him in the cave. Life was fine there. There were no beatings, and I slept well. She would come and sit on the edge of my bed and put her hand on my heart, and nothing more. Great quantities of fish, and I was very happy. Amigo Stettner, in the year 1980 a young professor

42

of the American School of Tangier came to my house. Mrabet, he said, some exchange students have arrived from America, and they would like to know you. They want to ask you questions, and hear you tell a story or two. With the greatest of pleasure, I told him. At four on Tuesday, I'll be here. Good-bye. Good-bye. They came at four; I opened the door and greeted the professor. There were seven students, another young man, and the professor, and an idiot with them who was their guide. And Amigo Stettner, the third girl I was introduced to was the girl from the sea. I greeted the others, but the only thing I could think of was that face. Is she the one? Could it be the same girl? Not possible. Yes, no, yes, no. And before she gave me her hand, she smiled, and it was exactly the same smile. I began to feel cold. They came in and sat down in the sala. Tea and cake. Amigo Stettner, that girl, whose name is Lindbergh, and whom I call Hadija, eventually gave me a small painting she had done here in Tangier. When I saw it, I liked it, because it was of an eye weeping. And very well drawn, fantastic. And the story I made about the weeping eye is for her. Thanks to all, and good-bye, hasta Dios quiere, and much good luck to everybody, and to you.

Mohammed Mrabet

Casa Zugari, Calle Ajdir,
Merstakhoche,
Tangier, Morocco.
2/vi/80

Querido Amigo Stettner:

       I hope you will forgive me for not writing in such a long time. I shut myself into the house for several weeks, during which time I made a lot of drawings, with colors. The work that took me the longest was a play I was recording. And of course friends would come to my house and find me doing that, and they would say: You're suffering a lot, Mrabet. I would reply: Of course. By suffering you mean working. But I've always liked the idea of having an extra book ready. That is, before number one is published, number two is already done. In this way the publisher will always be pleased. Amigo Stettner, you've been in my thoughts a lot, but I say to myself: he won't be angry if I don't write. Because I've got too much to do. And when I finish working at home I can't go out and visit Paul because I've smoked so much I'm not able to move. If I knew how to write, I could record while I was writing to you. And many thanks, amigo Stettner, for your great letter, and for number fifteen of <u>Stroker</u>. I liked it, and many of my friends liked it. And please give my thanks to your great friend Tommy Trantino. I liked his drawings. Anyone who doesn't understand the lives of other people as well as his own life is not going to be able to understand his drawing. In my mind, I see that man in the darkness, put there without deserving to have been put there. I know very well what governments are like, and what the police are like. The most savage people you'll see in your life. We can't do anything against that. It will all arrange itself one day. Many greetings to Tommy Trantino, with much will-power and a boiling heart. If it cools off, it's fatal. Amigo Stettner, I'm running back and forth and up and down now for my passport. And I think maybe I'll have it within ten days. And if I get it, I swear to you by my mother's milk that I'll visit you. I haven't seen New York since 1961. Even though everything has changed since then, I must go again and see the people who have been visiting me with their letters. And I'll be very happy. What I'd like most would be to find work there and not come back here, for two or three years. If I don't see anything in New York, from there I'll go directly to London. There I'm certain that I can find work, because there they want Moroccan cooks.

Amigo Stettner, life is not life. When the lips smile, the heart is not smiling. When I go to the market and make a large purchase and return home, I prepare everything with my two hands: tajine of chicken or meat, fish, salads, everything. I begin to eat, and it all tastes bitter to me. There can be others sitting with me eating, and I'm unable to eat. I smoke a lot. Much kif. Liters of coffee to drink with it. I can't drink alcohol. Amigo Stettner, if I drink alcohol, I swear to you I'll go to jail for twenty years. I smoke, and it calms me, cools me off. I've smoked for thirty years, and that's a long time.

Amigo Stettner, I don't know where I am. That is, I'm not tranquil. Something makes me move and run this way and that way. Let's say it doesn't matter. Perhaps all this motion will change me in some way, so I'll be different afterward.

Amigo Stettner, my new book, The Beach Café and The Voice, arrived. I liked the way it looked. A week after it came, I sent Black Sparrow a new book, Married with Papers. And soon I'll send him the play I'm doing.

Amigo Stettner, perhaps you won't believe what I'm going to tell you. I have a son; his name is Mohammed Larbi and he's eight years old. When he comes out of school, he doesn't go to his grandmother's house where his mother lives. He comes to see me. He has sixteen stories recorded on tape. I'd like to tell you one of them:

A man who was seventy-five years old had passed his whole life in the mountains, cutting trees. One day he was cutting down a very old olive tree. It was several hundred years old. He was hitting it with his axe, and a man came out of the trunk. And the man said: That's enough noise! You've been fifty-five years in this forest, and you've cut down half the trees. Every day I get a headache listening to your noise. Tell me, have you got a family?

No.

Are you married?

I've never been married.

Good. I'll give you something, and you'll go and get married. And the first year you'll have a son. And that son will be mine. The day he's born you've got to bring him here to me. All right?

Yes.

The man of the tree gave the woodcutter a lot of gold,

and the old man went away and got married. And the first year he had a son. He wrapped the baby up in a cloth and carried it to the man in the tree and gave it to him. The man took it and went back inside the tree, and the woodcutter returned to his wife.

She asked him: Where's the baby?

Her husband said: Oh, I promised it to a man who lives inside a tree in the forest.

What? she yelled. It's my baby, not yours!

It's our son, he told her. And that man made me rich.

No man can make another rich, she said. I want my son. Show me the tree where you took him.

Come on, he said.

And they went to the forest until they came to the tree.

How did you make the man come out of the tree? she wanted to know.

I was cutting the tree down.

They went home. The next morning the woman went out into the forest with the axe. She began to pound at the tree with it. After a half hour the man came out.

You want to get rich, too? he said to her.

No, sidi, she said. I want my son.

I bought him from your husband, he said.

My husband only has the right to sell you a baby from his own womb, she told the man. I suffered many months with that baby, and when he was born it nearly killed me. And now you've got to give him to me. What you do to my husband is between you two. If you don't give him up, I'll burn the whole forest down. I won't leave one tree.

He looked at her and said: I can see you'd do even more than that. I'll give your son. And I'll arrange with your husband later.

When you give me my son, if you want to make a tajine out of my husband, it's all the same to me.

The man went inside the tree and brought out the baby and gave it to the woman. She went home with it. Her husband was in the house when she arrived.

What! You've got the baby!

Yes, she said. And he gave me a big chest full of gold. But it's too big for me to carry. He's waiting for you at the tree.

He is? And the man ran off to the forest. The man was

waiting for him by the tree.

When he saw the woodcutter, he said: What do you want?

I came for the chest of gold.

The tree man grabbed the woodcutter and carried him inside the tree.

The woman took the baby and what gold was left, and went home to her family.

Amigo Stettner, adios, and another time adios.
With much good luck and much light shining, hasta Dios quiere,

Mohammed Mrabet

(*Stroker 17*, page 32)   Merstakhoche, Tangier,
                                           Morocco
                                           17/vi/80

Friend Trantino:[8]

       I greet you from Tangier. And I write this letter from my heart, because our friend Stettner has spoken to me about you in his letters, and I've seen your drawings in his magazine, and liked them.

       Amigo Trantino, I'd like to tell you something that happened to me when I was fifteen. A friend and I were on the boulevard in Tangier. My friend had twenty-five pesetas in his pocket. I didn't have anything. We went and bought two liters of wine. That cost six pesetas. And we bought some tapas to go with it, and a little kif. And we went and sat under some trees, and we stayed there; drinking and smoking. When the two bottles were empty, what with the kif we had smoked, we were well arranged in our heads. I said: Why don't we look for two women? He said: All right. We walked until we were near the Restaurant Paname. There we saw four girls. Amigo Trantino, I began to talk with them. I saw that they felt like having a good time. I said to them: Why don't you come with us to our mahal? We have everything there. They said yes. Two of them were Spanish and two were Moroccan Jewish girls. They came with us to our mahal. We went in. I sat with the girls while my friend went out to the baqal to buy what we needed. He bought all kinds of food. When he came back and we were in the kitchen, I said to him: But you didn't have any money. He said: I left a gold ring and a gold bracelet there with the baqal. Everyone ate and got drunk, and we made love with all four, amigo Trantino. But some informer had seen the girls with us, and had followed us to the mahal and gone away again. At half past two in the morning it sounded as though somebody were breaking down the door of the mahal. When I opened it, six men stood out there. What's going on? they said. We're going to take the girls with us. My friend ran out to them and said: You'll take them only if I'm lying here dead. Amigo Trantino, at quarter of three in the morning there were two lying dead there. And others badly

---

[8] Tommy Trantino is a writer and artist who was in state prison in New Jersey for 37 years. He came to Mrabet's attention through Irving Stettner and <u>Stroker</u> magazine. His best known work is <u>Lock The Lock</u>, 1973 (Alfred A. Knopf, Inc., NYC).

injured. We helped the girls escape, and my friend and I escaped too. But I went one way and he went the other, and they caught him on the boulevard. They gave him twenty years because they knew he was the one who had done it. But he stayed in jail
only fourteen years because he studied every day and was intelligent. Amigo, in our country they can't put people in jail unless they know exactly what happened. Everything is good, my friend. If I go to the United States, I want to visit you. I'll get our friend Stettner to take me.
As I am writing this letter I don't feel well. The pains come from a fall I had last week; I fell between two cliffs at the edge of the Atlantic. My head, my arms, my legs were all opened up. We know we're in the world to suffer.

Adios, hasta Dios quiere
with much luck and power, and much fire
in the heart.

Mohammed Mrabet

Merstakhoche, Tangier,
                                        Morocco.
                                        6/vii/80

Amigo Stettner:

          This letter is to bid you good afternoon, and to ask your
pardon for not having written for such a long time. I go a great deal to the
ocean, where I fish day or night. Now it is very hot. I'm already black.
There are many tourists. Wherever you go there are mounds of them.
Many English, many Germans, and many of other tribes. The beaches are
full, wherever you go. A dozen different beaches. The longest one is forty-
five kilometers from one end to the other. Full of people. The ocean is
depressed, because so many bodies shouldn't touch its water. So it is sad;
those bodies disgust it. Amigo Stettner, I'm doing a new kind of work. I
sent off a play called Earth. And the earth is the best thing. Now I'm doing
another play. Amigo Stettner, I'm going to tell you a small tale, for all our
friends. It's about a young man without a family who was left enough to
live on by his father when he died. With what he had he made a little
more. He fell in love with a girl and went to her father to ask for her. But
they were asking a fortune for her. He paid the sum they demanded, and
they arranged to hold the wedding in two weeks time. During the first
week he was taking a walk by himself, and he saw his future bride under
the trees being kissed by a man. He went up to them and said to her: What
are you doing? Nothing, she said. What do you mean? You were kissing
him. That's nothing, she said. That's the fashion nowadays. He said to her:
I worked for ten years, and all I saved I'm going to lose. And you think
you're going to make a fool of me in front of people, I'll kill you. He took
hold of her neck with one hand. The man with her tried to defend her, but
he found the young man's other hand around his neck. Amigo Stettner,
when he opened his hands, the two bodies fell onto the ground. They had
no more life in them. He went straight to the police, and said: I've killed
two people. Amigo Stettner, they called him to the tribunal, where they
gave him twenty years only, because he had right on his side. They put
him alone into a cell. Several years went past. One night he heard a
strange little sound. He got up and walked around the cell. Finally he
found a few large ants. He picked them up and put them into a little box.
Then he began to work with them, and went on working with them for

several years. Out of all the ants, only two remained alive. They were very large ants. Whatever commands he gave them they obeyed. He gave them dancing lessons. They could stand on two legs like people, and give each other their claws. He taught them to make sounds. And he would put a little food on a small dish, and they would go and eat. He would open the box, and they would climb back in and hide. Amigo Stettner, all the years left to pass in jail, he passed with the ants.

I've lost everything, he would say to himself, and when I get out of here I'm not going to have anywhere to sleep. And he said to himself: Soon I'm going to get out, and I'll earn my living with the ants. He was let out of prison, and he went directly to a café to order a black coffee. The waiter brought the coffee to his table. Wait a minute, he told the waiter. I'm going to show you something interesting. He brought out the little box and set it on the table, and opened it. He called twice, and the two ants came out. The waiter was not watching. The ants began to walk on the table, and he gave them the order to stand up. Amigo Stettner, when the ants were ready to dance, the waiter suddenly looked down at the table and saw them. Then he brought his hand down hard on them and crushed them, and swept them off the table. What was it you wanted to show me? he said. The owner of the ants jumped up and seized the waiter by the neck. When he let go, the waiter was dead. The police came and took him away. How does it happen that today you finished serving twenty years, and now you're going to serve another twenty? they asked him, laughing. They passed him through the tribunal. He explained everything, and they told him: All right, we'll give you some of the same kind of ants, and you'll be in your cell, and when the ants begin to dance, you can call for us. They shut him into the prison and gave him what he needed. Yes, amigo Stettner, in a few years he had taught four large ants to do the same things the others had done. And he sent word to the government; I'm ready to show my ants. They took him to a big palace where he showed them all how his ants could dance and bow. And the government gave him his freedom and restored what had been confiscated from him many years before. Amigo Stettner, I send you many greetings. Adios, hasta Dios quiere.

Mohammed Mrabet

(*Stroker 17*, page 8)   Merstakhoche, Tangier,
                                                          Morocco.
                                                          13/vii/80

Querido Amigo Stettner:

        Let us chat a bit. I can't ever write to you unless I'm kiffed. If it weren't for kif I'd do nothing; I wouldn't write letters or books, or draw pictures. I'd be an old man in a corner if I didn't smoke. Thank you for the copies of <u>Stroker</u> 16. And thank you too for the copy you sent to the señorita. Amigo Stettner, I've done a lot of work this year. I have almost four books ready. I've drawn a hundred and thirty pictures in black and white and in color. I'll send you one of the new ones. Now I'm busy doing a second play, and I hope to finish it shortly. Amigo Stettner, I saw him running on top of the trees, like a dragon. Running day and night, and fire comes out of his mouth. Neither water nor earth is of any use against him. It's a pity. He's burned everything, and he looks happy. It's only because of a fly that he's stopped breathing fire. He sleeps now by day and wanders at night. When they asked him about it, he answered: I like the darkness. There's no difference between day and night. But the night is sweeter than the day. The writers who are people and the poets, and all people who are people understand what the night means. And better if there is hashish, magic music, words of fantasy. Like the King and the Queen floating in the air. Amigo Stettner, there were some Americans and Englishmen discussing the various kinds of food there are in the world. They asked me which food I liked best, and I said there were two. What are they? they asked me. Hashish and love, I told them. They looked at me and said: You're crazy. And I began to laugh, and said: Thank you. Adios, hasta Dios quiere. Good luck,

                    Mohammed Mrabet

Casa Zugari, Calle Ajdir,
Merstakhoche,
Tangier, Morocco
16/viii/80

Amigo Stettner:

I'm writing you seriously. I'm going to tell you something new, because it's natural that each year brings all kinds of new things. And everything is always changing. There are people living in the world who never think of the years going past. Amigo Stettner, it is necessary to think of life, and think of the year one is living in. Everything is constantly moving. The earth changes, and everything which grows changes. And people, even those who think they are eternal, change and become something else from what they were. In my country there is no difference between the white race and the black race. The difference there is among us is the amount we earn. Each one is paid according to the work he does. The closest friend of the Prophet was Billal, the great muezzin, and he was very black. I have many black friends here. Amigo Stettner, the blacks who live in California are intelligent, and I think they haven't forgotten anything. The gangster-governor of California was rough with them, and his name was Reagan. There are many people who know how to clean plates with their tongues. And people know that this man is the friend of the men with the greatest fortunes. Let's hope he doesn't become the president. If he does, adios America! The shell began to crack when Kennedy was shot. And if the gangster wins, the whole egg will spill out and that will be good-bye. Amigo Stettner, all this means nothing to me, because I'm far away. Only when I hear the news and see the magazines, my heart aches. It makes me feel sorry for the poor people and the ones who have no power or strength. All this makes me very nervous, and I'd like to hear that such people are content. Amigo Stettner, I had a dream unlike any other I'd had before; if I hadn't had it, I couldn't have imagined it. I arrived at my house at half past ten in the evening. I went in and turned on the light. I put some water on the fire and made some coffee. I smoked, drank the coffee, and finished a drawing that needed a little more work on it. Then I got up and went to bed. I was asleep. In my dream I found myself in a countryside made only of sand and boulders. I was thirsty and I was looking for water. I sat on a big rock looking up and down. I had no shoes and my trousers were ragged. When I looked at my chest, for I had no shirt either, I saw that I was covered with hair. I have no hair on my chest. Then I saw a headless torso walking past. And behind it there were two small children running, carrying in their hands vessels to fetch water. Catch him, sir, please! they shouted to me. He's going to leave us without any water! And when I heard the word <u>water</u>, I got up and ran after the torso and caught it around the waist with my arms. Then I heard the two children behind me calling: Look out! Look out! When I turned to look, I saw the head moving along the ground with it's mouth open, ready to bite my leg. I put my foot on the head, and it said to me: What do you want? I said: I want water, for me and for those two children. The head told me: I have no water. All I have is food. I said: We're not hungry. We want water. Then the month opened even wider, and a stream of water poured out of it. I kept pushing hard on the head with my foot, and the head began to sink into the ground, and the water came out in greater quantity, and the head finally disappeared. Then I put the torso on top of the spot where the head had buried itself, and it too sank into the ground. And the water poured out day and night. Something bit me and when I opened my eyes, it was a mosquito. Amigo Stettner, adios. Hasta Dios quiere.

Mucha suerte

Mohammed Mrabet

(Stroker 18, page 6)   Merstakhoche,
                                          Tangier, Morocco
                                          24/ix/80

Amigo Stettner:

           Thank you for your good letters. They came at a
moment when I was drowning. I felt very sick, very sad. My whole body
ached. I couldn't sleep at night at all. And I was running up and down all
day. It doesn't matter. Amigo Stettner, I'm going to send you a long story,
all by itself. It isn't a letter. And you can publish it if you have room for it.
And with that story I'll send you at the same time the drawing in color I
promised you a long time ago. I committed a fault by not sending it to you
before this, I know. I'm nervous day and night. I don't know what I'm
doing. I smoke about three hundred grams of hash each day. Amigo
Stettner, I've lost a second mother. I would spend my time with her, and
much more time than I'd spend with my own mother. She helped me with
half of my life. I can't forget her. She was my wife's mother. My wife has
always hated me, and her mother always loved me. She was the woman
who gave me a great importance. She thought me more important than her
own children. An old woman of seventy years. A fantastic woman. Amigo
Stettner, in the beginning that woman hated me too, because people talked
too much. When she saw that the gossip wasn't exact, she changed. One
day she found me very ill, and she thought I was going to die, and she
came and said to me: Forgive me for what went on in the past, for it was
an error. And I said to her: Yes, I forgive you, because it's not your fault.
You're a woman of the mountains and you've never studied. Yes, I
forgive you. And from that day on, she placed me firmly inside her heart.
And I put her inside my eyes. She had wealthy children who would arrive
in Morocco and ask her: Do you want to go somewhere? She would say:
Yes, I want to go and visit a certain saint, but I won't go until Mrabet
comes. Amigo Stettner, it's all true; there's no invention. I'm very, very
sad. Day before yesterday she died at half past seven in the morning. Five
days before she died, she spoke, and she said: I want you to treat Mrabet
as I've treated him. I love him very much, and I've always preferred him
to all of you, even though I love you more than anything. I know that all
my children are dutiful. Every one of you has treated me like a queen, and
I've lived like a queen. Well, not one of you has taken such care of me as

Mrabet. My medicines, my food, my house. He takes care of all the gold and jewelry in the house. I've seen that he always spends his own money when he comes here to eat. I'm very much attached to him. And she said no further words. I went there in the morning, and before I got to the house my heart changed, my skin rose up in pinfeathers, and the water flowed inside my eyes. When I got outside the door there were many small children standing there. I ran, and went inside the house, and there was the whole family weeping. She had just died a moment before. I went directly into her room, pulled down the sheet that covered her face, and put three kisses on her forehead. Her face was still warm. But it was completely yellow, with tinges of green. I pulled the sheet up again and became white as the walls, trembling.

Amigo Stettner, they said to me: You must go and tell Ahmed that mother has died. I went and I said to him: Your mother is dead. He said: She died? And I said: Yes. Do you want me to help you? Amigo Stettner, when that woman died, I said to myself: Things aren't going to go right any more. And I was right, because when I asked her son if he wanted me to help him, he replied: I don't need anybody's help. I heard him, and I paid no attention. I went back to the house and gave the money to make the grave, and I helped through the entire ritual, up until we buried her. Amigo Stettner, that's the way life is: you are conceived, you are born, and you die. Yes, Amigo Stettner. Also I was given a year of prison and 2,500 dirhams fine. It's my wife who wants to see me in jail even though I haven't done anything. What did I do? A book, a novel, all about it, and Black Sparrow has it. With this suspended sentence hanging over me, there's nothing I can do. When she heard that I had a passport, she began to play Charlie Chaplin games with me. If only she had been really Charlie Chaplin! He was something fantastic. She wants them to take my passport away from me, or she wants to provoke me to such a degree that I'll do something which would be punishable with a long jail sentence. Amigo Stettner, adios, hasta Dios quiere. Good luck and a long life to you and to our friends. And many greetings to whatever friend of yours asks after me.

Mohammed Mrabet

Casa Zugari, Calle Ajdir,
Merstakhoche, Tangier,
Morocco.
26/x/80

Amigo Stettner:

Thank you for your good letter. With this present letter I'm sending you a small drawing and a larger one. Amigo Stettner, I'm waiting day after day for a chance to leave Tangier. I'm thinking of going with a friend to Barcelona or Madrid, to sell things. I have many stamps from many countries from a century ago, and I'd like to see if they can offer me a good price. The friend will take antique silver coins with him. Amigo Stettner, I'm telling you the truth: there's no way I can know what I'm doing. I'm lost. I'm very much afraid. Afraid of doing something horrible without thinking first. At this moment I'm lost. I don't like to go to jail without having done anything. Sometimes I can't even breathe. I begin to tremble, and I get as cold as a frigidaire. I don't like arriving at that point of trouble. Amigo Stettner, here in Tangier it has rained a little. The beaches are very clean, and there's nobody on them. There's only a big Land Rover with two men and two women from Florida. A few days ago I met them, because they came and bought a few fish from me. When I had sold them a large fish for twenty-five dollars, they were looking at each other. What's happening? I asked them. They asked me about Ketama in the Rif, and I said: What do you want to do up there? We just want to go there, they said. Do you want to come with us? Thanks, but I can't, I said. They wanted to know why I couldn't. There's too much jasmine there, I said. But jasmine smells wonderful, they said. Yes, but it gives me a headache, I told them. Amigo Stettner, I thought I smoke more kif than anybody, but it isn't true. I've watched those Americans. They smoke it and they eat it. And they carry a white powder they put up their noses. What they had that interested me most was a large stereo machine with Bob Marley and Peter Tosh. Amigo Stettner, I've never spoken to you about my great friend the fish. This fish takes good care of me. When I'm alone in my house he comes to visit me. When I mention him to my friends, of course they think I've gone crazy. But I'm not crazy, and I can see the fish and he speaks to me. He always brings me the latest news. The thing I most like about him is that when I'm busy doing a story or a novel, and can't find the right ending for it, he comes and says a few words that open the way for me, and I go ahead and finish the work. This is the first time I've spoken to you about the fish. I thought of mentioning it before, but then I thought you might think I was making fun of you by telling such a thing.

Amigo Stettner, thank you for everything. We must meet sometime. Adios, hasta Dios quiere, and greetings to all our friends. Good luck.

Mohammed Mrabet

Morocco
                                                    9/xi/80

Amigo Stettner:
                I'm writing this letter to say thank you, for your kind
gift. I sent you some drawings I made many years ago. As you can see,
they're not like the ones I do now.
                I'm trying to do this letter, and without being able to
talk very well. I had two molars taken out. When I saw them I realized that
they weren't human teeth, but donkey's teeth. Of course my face is very
swollen, and one eye is swelled up, too. And my teeth go right on aching. I
mean those that are still there.
                Amigo Stettner, I have some new stories by my boy. He
escapes from his mother and comes to see me. I can see that he wants to
be something. He arrives at my house and begins to tell stories. He told me
one he has on tape, and I believe that if life is long enough I'll make a
book out of his stories. In this tale there's a Belgian doctor who came to
Tangier and set up a small office where people could come and consult
him. When some sick person would arrive, he would ask that person
questions. Then he would take out a big book and begin to look through it.
He finally got a job in a big hospital, where he performed operations. One
night he was working there in the hospital. There was a woman there who
had been trying for two days to give birth to a baby. The doctor decided
that she needed an operation. They took the woman to the operating room.
The doctor changed his clothes and came in. He cut her open and pulled
out the baby alive. The woman was all right, too. Her husband worked in
London, and after a few months she began to write to him saying that she
had pains. Soon he came to Tangier and took her away to London with
him. There he made her see a doctor. When they had taken x-rays of her,
they found a glove of rubber inside. It was something the Belgian doctor
had left by mistake. They performed another operation, and the doctor said
that if she had left it there she could have had a cancer. Amigo Stettner,
Paul is copying the story I promised to send you. There is no good copy of
it. I'm going to send it very soon. And I'll also send you a drawing in
color, not from ten years ago. Tangier looks clean because it has been
raining for a few days, and that makes the streets look like new, and the
walls, and even some people. Because there is a kind of people who hate
water. They get wet only when it's raining or if they happen to fall into a

river somewhere. Tangier is constantly growing larger, thanks to the money of the Saudis and the Kuwaitis. Rich people come to live in our country, and up go the prices of everything. A pack of Marlboros costs two dollars now. Amigo Stettner, I'm still thinking of going to visit you. You can understand why I haven't yet arrived there. I'd like to go and see you, and also see a great friend of mine. I can tell you her name, and she'll forgive me. She is called Clara Jacob, and she lives in New York. She spent a month and a half in Tangier. She is one of Paul's students. And she told me stories which interested me. Amigo Stettner, I know this letter is short, but I'm very very tired. Adios, hasta Dios quiere. Much luck to you and all your friends,

Mohammed Mrabet

Morocco
                                                    11/xii/80

Amigo Stettner:

          Many salutations and much hot chile. I'm writing from
inside my heart. In our tchar in the Rif they say of a man who works hard:
He's a man full of hot peppers. I ask your pardon for not having written
you recently. Amigo Stettner, I've bought a piece of land out in the
country, instead of going to New York. And I borrowed a little more in
order to pay for the lawyers and registration. I've been working for two
months, very hard. I get up at five in the morning. At quarter past six I'm
on the land. That's when it begins to be day. I have many olive trees.
There are many birds, and the air smells good. I'm trying to get a tiny
shack built, and I'm planting everywhere. When spring comes I'll be
waiting to see if somebody comes to visit me, and we can sit under a trellis
of canes and amuse ourselves as we like. There are four kilometers
between my land and the airport. Amigo Stettner, I've decided to stop
making books, because I haven't the time for it. When it gets to be eight
o'clock in the evening, all I want to do is sleep. Fifteen days of working
ten hours a day, and fifteen days of working eight, splitting boulders,
sawing enormous cactuses off at the ground, digging up their roots, tearing
down blackberry brambles. I've dug a deep well. Now there are about two
hundred tons of stones lying in piles around the property. With those
stones I'm building walls to shore up the earth, as it lies on a steep hill.
Amigo Stettner, I swear, if you stand there on my property, you won't
think you're near Tangier. You'll think you're in Colorado or Arizona.
There are several Americans living nearby. One above and one below. But
we're far from each other, and they keep their horses in stables. I'm very
happy with the place, and that's why I'm working so hard. I hope I'll be
able to live out there when spring comes. Each morning I see animals:
rabbits, hares, hedgehogs and tortoises. Many kinds of birds of all sizes
and colors. I'm surrounded by trees. And when the sun comes up over the
mountains, it hits me in the face immediately.
          Well, Amigo Stettner, I'll send you a photo of the place
as it was when I bought it, and another showing it as it is. When I was one
year old, my grandmother put hot chile in my mouth. I cried for half a day,
and was angry the other half. When they asked her why she'd done that,
she said: So that when he grows to be a man, he'll know how to take care

of himself. And she was right, Amigo Stettner. When I was ten or eleven I always imagined I was a man of twenty. Yes, Amigo Stettner, I'm forty now, and I imagine I'm eighty. So I act like a man of eighty, and this keeps everyone from bothering me. I left off smoking hash, and have gone back to smoking kif as I always used to, and in a pipe I've had for twenty years.

Amigo Stettner, soon I'll write you again. You are one of my best friends in America, and you deserve a better letter than this. If you ever think of coming to Tangier, you must absolutely not think of going to a hotel. There are three places where you can stay. You can have my house in Tangier. Or you can stay in the country, with me. Or you can stay at my mother's, where you'd have the second floor. I don't believe I can go to America this year. Adios. Good luck. Greetings to you and all your friends.

Mohammed Mrabet

Casa Zugari, Calle Ajdir,
Merstakhoche, Tangier,
Morocco.
23 i 81

Dear Friend Stettner:

Many greetings and embraces. Many thanks for Stroker 17 which you sent me. Marvelous! I like you and everything you do. Amigo Stettner, there is fear in Tangier. It hasn't rained yet. There's no water. Day after day, week after week, only bright sun. When I get up at half past five in the morning, I look at the sky and become happy all by myself, because the sky is covered with clouds. And I say: it's going to rain. And when I arrive out at my property in the country and begin to work, perhaps in the middle of the morning, the sun burns away the clouds and hits me. Then I go underneath an olive tree and sit in the shade. The trees I've planted need water. And my well is empty of all but a very little water. A little sad. Amigo Stettner, here's something that happened to me. I have a shelter where I keep my sheep. I went in there to sharpen an axe, to get at some trees I wanted to cut. As I went in I heard a strange sound, and when I turned on a flashlight there were three lambs lying there, very dirty because they had only just been born. And their mothers were busy licking them so they would be clean. When they finished I took them out of that shelter and put them in another place. There were two families. There was also a male, but it was born dead.

Amigo Stettner, I go on working and taking care of the animals. I've worked at all kinds of business, and I never earned anything with them. Now I'm trying out the business of our forefathers, working on the earth. But it takes a lot of money at the beginning. Did you ever receive the drawings in color I sent you? I don't know whether they arrived in New York or not. Amigo Stettner, there were girls who wrote me last year. I notice that none of them writes any more. It's not necessary to give you their names. You know them better than I. I don't know whether my letters frightened them, or the idea of writing back and forth. I always write letters without thinking, and often I wonder if I've made an error, but I tell myself that the friend I'm writing to will understand and make allowances for my mistake. Amigo Stettner, I've received many letters containing great insults, and I never was angry. I stayed my normal self. And I would write to the person who had insulted me, a friendly letter, saying Dear Friend, I am not the son of a whore. I know both my mother and my father. Yes, I knew my father very well. My mother started to go out of the house alone only when I was already married. I went on to say that I knew a little story that would interest him. I said there was a man, a very rich man, who had three sons. He called them in, and they sat down with their father, who said to them: My sons, now you are grown up. I'm going to distribute your inheritance among you while I'm still alive. And the sons said: Why father?

I want to see if you're of my own blood, or if you're of another's blood, he told them. He had spent his life making long voyages away from home.

The sons agreed. The old man took money out of the chest where he piled it. There were a million reales, and the father gave each son a quarter of a million. Each one of you has a house, and I'm staying here in mine. Good-bye. The sons married and took their wives to their houses. Each day there were parties and quests. Everyone was drunk. The three sons began to do, my friend, what your father did to your mother in France. Your father would get drunk, and your mother would get drunk, and they would get angry with each other. Your father would go out with another woman, while your mother went out with another man. The three sons exchanged wives, and everybody slept with everybody. Can you tell me, my friend, which one was your father, the one who was with your mother or the one who was out with the other woman? My mother had no time, because every year another child was born. When I was six years old, there were five younger than me. And my father had no time, either. He had two wives and twenty-four children; each wife gave him twelve. The poor man had no time to go to restaurants or dance halls. At least, I knew my father very well. And you, my friend, one should take pity on you because you know you're a bonafide son of a whore, and knowing that, you accuse others of being the same as you. Your friend …

Amigo Stettner, that particular friend had spent a month with me here in Tangier. At that time I had a little shack beside the sea. He had arrived, and he had no money, and I gave the place to him so he'd have a place to live, and he stayed for a month. And now he's paying me back with insults! Amigo Stettner, I'm trying to put together a book of stories. I don't know how many there are. Perhaps fifteen. And I'm also finishing a novel. The work I had to do on my land is far from finished.

And when I get through with that I hope to have time to do my own work, drawing and recording stories.

Well, Amigo Stettner, I'm thankful I didn't fly to New York. Recently I saw a book of photographs of New York the way it looks today. I thought it was some place in Africa like Angola or Libya, or Algeria. I couldn't believe it was New York. When I was in New York, people didn't sell rags in the street. They didn't fill the sidewalk with boxes full of junk for sale. When I was in New York, it was a fantastic city. There were gangs, yes, groups of teenagers. Many Porto Riquenos and other Latins. But it wasn't anything very important. I spent many wonderful nights in New York. You could go where you wanted in Harlem, you could wander where you wanted, all over Brooklyn. I lived at 25 West Central Park, and when I went out, I always aimed straight at either Harlem or Brooklyn, because those were the most amusing sections of the city. I had a few young black friends, and they were fantastic, too. And now, New York looks like garbage. Amigo Stettner, all my condolences for the new president you now have. The new invalid. People living in poverty. Is he going to help the poor? All he seems to want is a bigger army. He and his wife want people in America to buy more guns, so they can all kill each other. Has he thought of something good? All this is sad. There's a saying: <u>Men</u> <u>ez</u> <u>zebbala</u> <u>al</u> <u>taifor</u>. "He has come to the table directly from the garbage pail." (That is, to say, without washing.) I'm a movie star, my son is a dancer, and my daughter a singer. But my wife is a Madame. Adios, hasta Dios quiere. Much luck, good health, and incha'Allah (God Willing) we can see one another some day. That day I'll make you explode with laughter.

Mohammed Mrabet

(*Stroker 19*, page 26)
Merstakhoche, Tangier,
Morocco.
15 ii 81

Dear Friend Stettner:

Many salutations from Tangier! I think what I'm going to tell you will please you. A young man who is born with eyes, and can see, at ten years of age becomes blind. He has no family. Only a large room which is something like a café, where his friends can come and see him. They make tea there, and food. They eat and drink tea and smoke kif together, and the blind youth tells stories, and these are all about what he can see. He says he can see all kinds of things in front of his eyes. Not far from his room lives the wealthiest girl in the city. She often sees him in the street, and she has fallen in love with him. Then she discovers that she can see him through the window if she walks in her father's garden. And she can also hear all the tales he tells to his friends. Amigo Stettner, the young man who was blind said: I've seen hell, and I saw it for a year and a month. Thousands of people suffering. Alive in the flames. Alive and drinking what they thought was water. But it was only fire. Millions of people in the fire, and still alive. He said that he had been in the slaughterhouse for a year and four months. He had spent three months longer because it was a little more interesting. There were many varieties of liver, heart and kidneys there, and great quantities of chops. And rivers of blood. Thousands of people hanging on hooks and cut into strips. The blind young man said he had been to Paradise, and there he had spent five years. It was still more interesting, he said, and much prettier. The air smelled of roses and jasmine and carnations and orange blossoms. Canals of water running in many directions, and everything very clean. And he said that in Paradise he ate well and slept well, and saw only things that were good, so that he was able to forget all the others that had not been. He said: I put my face beside the window and I saw a girl in love. How can that be? said his friends. I'm not lying, he told them. I've seen a girl outside the window, and she's in love. Then, you can see? they said. No, I can't see, he said, but I can feel. I can feel what's good and what isn't. I've been able to do that since the day I was blind.

Amigo Stettner, the young man said to all his friends who were with him: is there anyone here who can look for two seconds into my eyes? No, they said. There isn't anybody who can do that.

Whoever talks to you keeps his eyes lowered. Amigo Stettner, when we do the translation of this play, I'll send you a copy. And if the drawings I sent you still haven't arrived, along with a copy of <u>Blades,</u> a tiny magazine which had a letter from Henry Miller to me in it, let me know and I'll send some other drawings.

   Today was the first day of the winter that it has rained. Let us hope it keeps on raining for three or four days, day and night. Because the earth needs some water very badly. And the trees have had no rain since last spring. And the wells are empty, and the animals need water to drink. Amigo Stettner, I'm trying to make a large book of stories. I have some that are already translated, and others which are not. Amigo Stettner, you must think of me exactly as you think of yourself, because I'm very fond of you. I think you're capable only of good things. Adios, hasta Dios quiere. Much luck and power and a long life and friendship that lasts until the end.

        Mohammed Mrabet

Casa Zugari, Calle Ajdir,
Merstakhocke, Tangier,
Morocco.
2/iii/81

Dear Amigo Stettner:

Many greetings and regards. And the same to all our friends. I'm happy to be writing you this note. The work I'm doing out in the country is making me skid, and I'm very much afraid of crashing. I can't even sleep well. I don't worry about two or three things, but about dozens of things. This very morning early, I was out there in the country. I fed my two dogs, Django and Tony. And afterwards I gave water to eighty-five little trees. Most of them have put out leaves now. It's too bad, Amigo Stettner, that there's no rain. I have a well, thanks to God, which has a little water in it each morning. I'm now ready to put the roof on the house. It will look like a house from long ago, I think. Maybe Roman, maybe Arab. Amigo Stettner, I ask your forgiveness for not writing you as often as before, but I haven't time. There are days when I don't want to speak to anyone or see anyone. Everything disgusts me on those days. It doesn't matter. Everything is fantastic.

Amigo Stettner, I received a fine gift today, from a great friend of mine. I've never spoken to you about him. He sent me a picture of a sheep, and any painter or any person who looks at it won't believe that it was done by hand. The great friend is Claudio Bravo. I'm delighted with the picture, because I've been seeing it for about eight years now, and I've always loved it. He has a fantastic talent. And he's also very generous and a great host. Two or three weeks ago we ate at his house, Paul and I, with a woman from Madrid who has a big art gallery there. Amigo Stettner, tomorrow is Tuesday. All over Morocco there will be a big festival in honor of our king. The Aid el Aarch.

All the cities will be shining with lights and draped with banners, and the streets will be full of parades. And many different kinds of music that one never hears in the street. All the Moroccans are in a state of joyfulness, and they all cry: Long Live the King!

Amigo Stettner, I love to be in my country. I've travelled, but I shouldn't want to exchange my land for another. I live in the center of the city. Outside, if I walk a few hundred meters I can find many trees. They tell me that in New York a man needs about two thousand dollars a month to live. And here where I am I can live on less than five hundred.

I'll send you two other drawings in color. There's no more confidence in the postal system. These days we're in festival, but in three or four days I'll send you the pictures. The other envelope was sent airmail registered (no. 058) on November 3rd from Tangier-Emsallah. I don't know which end made the trouble, but you say you haven't received it.

Amigo Stettner, good-bye. Hasta Dios quiere. Much luck.

Mohammed Mrabet

Merstakhoche, Tangier,
Morocco.
6/v/81

Querido Amigo Stettner:

I send many greetings and embraces. I know it has been a long time since I've written you. I spent almost a month feeling very ill, all this on account of one ear. I'll tell you how it happened. It rained very heavily one night, so much that I went out to my land. A stupid man who lives behind me, and who has never taken any care of his land, had let the water run from his land onto mine, and I had to work three or four hours that night in the cold downpour, digging channels where the water could run without ruining my garden. I sent the water around the outside of my land finally. Amigo Stettner, although it's shameful, I'm going to say it. The water soaked me completely, and the cold entered into my heart. I found it hard to breathe with the cold I felt. When I got back to Tangier I took off my clothes, dried myself and went back to bed. In the morning I couldn't get up. Many tears in my eyes, much water from my nostrils, and a noise in my ear like a train going past. And the ear got infected and my face swelled up on one side, and of course I had to go and visit a doctor. Two kilos of medicine. Two kilos of poison for my body to absorb. Amigo Stettner, now I'm better; I feel well once more. I ask your forgiveness for not having written you before this. And also I'm going to ask a favor of you, if you don't mind. I have a new friend from Spain; very intelligent translations into Spanish he makes. He has translated some of my stories from English into Spanish, and his work is perfect. He left with me a story of his. (He has published a novel in Spain.) He wanted to know if I would send this story of his to Stroker and I told him I would. I said: Good. Now Paul has it, and he's doing me the favor of translating it from Spanish into English. And if it interests you I'll send it to you.

Amigo Stettner, one night I took your photo and the photo of Henry Miller and one of Tennessee Williams and one of Paul Bowles and my own. I put them in a row in front of me and began to smoke. I have a handsome sebsi, I prepare my kif with my own hands; it's the cleanest possible. And I made a pot of tea with many herbs in it. I went on smoking, and put questions to each face in front of me. The first question I put to Tennessee. He looked at me in a way I didn't like, and said: You're fatally ill, Mrabet. The second question I put to Paul. What can I do? I asked him. He replied: The only thing you can do is stand it and go on standing it. The third question I asked of you, Amigo Stettner. What can I do? I asked you. You told me: Work a lot, so you can forget everything. The fourth question I asked myself. What can I do? I said to my face. And I answered myself: Mrabet, you must suffer. And the fifth question I asked of the friend I never saw, but will never forget, Henry Miller. What can I do, dear friend? I asked him. He smiled and said: There's nothing finer than death. You won't have to worry about anything. You won't hear anything, my dear Mrabet.

Amigo Stettner, I put the photographs back into their envelope, and invented a fantastic story. Amigo Stettner, the drawings and photo I sent you last autumn stayed a while in New York and came back here after five months, so now I have them. And this time it won't be like that. I'll send it again, and to the very same address, but perhaps they'll deliver it.

Adios, hasta Dios quiere. Good luck
and good health to you and to all
the friends.

Mohammed Mrabet

Tangier, Morocco.
18/v/81

Amigo Stettner:

Many greetings and embraces. I am very well; only a
little crazy. In the morning early I take out my sheep. At six I'm in the
country with the animals, eating. At one I put the animals into their sheds,
because the sun is very powerful and hot. Afterward I go with two
workmen to the orchard and begin to plant things. All varieties of
vegetables and many flowers. Tuberose, carnations, honeysuckle and
jasmine. And roses. The house is nearly finished. I'm very happy and in
good health. A little plumper.

Amigo Stettner, there are people who think they are
gods. We have a saying: An ant can damage a camel. In the life of a man
many things can happen. For example, there was a rich man with great
power, but he did nothing well. Whatever he did was badly done. When he
made a gift to someone, he accompanied it with insults. If he did
something for someone, he didn't do it because his heart told him to do it.
And when people came to ask favors of him, he didn't think of them as
real people, but only as shadows, because they were poor. His thoughts
were not in good order. If he had been able to think, he would have
realized that he lived thanks to those people. It was they who provided him
with all his money. Of course, pimps always have good luck. Amigo
Stettner, I tell you the truth, if I hadn't seen all this with my own eyes, I
couldn't write it to you. (I also saw in my dreams a man with a whip. He
was covered with blood, lying on the ground, with a black man standing
above him, holding a small machine-gun that shoots thirty bullets. I felt
very sorry for the young man, all the more because I didn't feel sorry at all
for the shot man.)

Amigo Stettner, the only person for whom I felt pity
was the young black man. In my dream, nine more like the one who was
shot needed to be shot. Later, if they were to execute the black, I wouldn't
be sorry, simply because ten had been shot instead of one. That was worth
it, I thought.

Amigo Stettner, Tangier is fine. All parts of Morocco
are fine, too. Eight of my younger brothers made a voyage through the
country. When they came back, each one told me his story. They found
everything wonderful. And they spent very little money. They ate and

slept well. It's true that everything is cheap here compared with Europe. If there they pay four or five hundred dollars a month for a house, here for the same price they could have a fine house furnished.

Amigo Stettner, I'll relate a short tale. I just heard it for the first time, from a boy of nine. There was a farmer who as he went into his house noticed some ants on the floor, and each one was carrying a grain of wheat. The man asked them: What are you doing? The biggest ant said: We're just taking some grains of wheat home, to have some food in the house. The farmer said: No, no. You're stealing, and you've got to come with me to the pacha. The ant said to the others: My sons, you go home. The sons went home and the big ant went with the farmer to see the pacha. They went before him, and he said: What is this? The farmer said: This ant and his sons were stealing wheat off my floor. The pacha said to the ant: And why were you stealing wheat? The ant said: We were only taking what had been left on the floor. The pacha said: One year of prison for the thief. And to the ant he said: How much food do you need a year? The ant answered: One grain of wheat. The pacha put the ant inside a bamboo tube, added one grain of wheat, and shut the tube. When the year was up, the pacha opened the bamboo tube and shook out the ant. And with it came half the grain of wheat. The pacha said to the ant: Didn't you say that you ate a whole grain of wheat in a year? The ant replied: I was afraid to eat the whole grain in case you forgot to open up the tube, and I thought I'd better leave half of it for the next year. The pacha said: Go home. But the ant said: No! The pacha asked the ant: What do you want? The ant said: You've got to come with me to the king. The pacha said: All right. So they went. When they stood before the king, he said to them: What is this? The ant spoke. Your majesty, a farmer left some grains of wheat lying on the floor in his house, and my sons and I began to clean up the floor and take away the grains. We're not the sort of ants who are always looking for food. We come outside only during the hot months. And the farmer said I was robbing him, and the pacha gave me a year of prison. A year, with one grain of wheat. I don't live only on wheat. I eat many other things as well. And I drink water, too.

The king turned to the pacha and said: What do you mean by this? The pacha said: That's the way it was. The king then said: Well, if that's the way it was, I sentence you to one year in jail. Which do you want, bread or water? The pacha said: Water. Then the ant whispered to the pacha: If all you have is water, you'll die. And if all you have is

76

bread, you'll die, too. But if you ask him for milk, you can live. The pacha spent a year in jail drinking milk. Amigo Stettner, adios, hasta Dios quiere, much good luck, and until very soon. Greetings to all the friends.

Mohammed Mrabet

Merstakhoche,
Tangier, Morocco
24/x/81

Querido Amigo Stettner:

      Many greetings and hugs. I'm very much lost, with many pains and sadnesses. I can't talk for very long at a time, I can't eat, I can't drink anything cold or hot. My whole body is poisoned. My throat is swollen, my eyes let tears run out, and I have a bad headache. I feel like being in bed all the time, like someone who takes drugs and never lets them leave his blood. Amigo Stettner, a week ago I went to Gibraltar; I flew over in the morning, bought a round-trip passage to London, and came back to Tangier. I'm going to have a small operation there. And besides, a strange swelling has come out on my arm. If it's necessary, I'll have that taken care of, too. On the twenty-eighth at three thirty in the afternoon I'll be in London. Amigo Stettner, life is disgusting. For people who have big hearts it's disgusting and discouraging. Everything which is happening and everything they're doing is their fault. They think they're doing good, but it's not true. Just the contrary. For instance, only in the year 1960 I was in New York, and I saw all of New York, all the crevices. I wandered along the good avenues and the dangerous ones. I stayed until three in the morning in Central Park drinking beer. In that era I was very young and healthy, and I liked sports more than anything else. There were young men, black and white, playing various games, and it was a pleasure to stand and watch them. Amigo Stettner, now that no longer exists. The young men I see, if they're not sick, are crazy. That's the way their fathers and grandfathers want it. Because the city has gone rotten and those who have the power in the city are rotten as well. And when they saw that the land had decayed the same as they had, they said to each other: Our sons and grandsons have got to be as rotten as everything else. Amigo Stettner, I'll write to you from London. If I can't write it in English, I'll write it all in Arabic. Because you know I can't write, at least in English. I can write a little in my own language, Arabic, however. I've never studied anything. If I had studied for years, I'd be a terrible man, one of the rotten ones, like all the others. How can a professor who has come out of a great university and is somebody of great importance belittle a man who never went to school? He doesn't even know him personally. Amigo Stettner, I swear to you that if this professor were beside me I could arrange his face in such a way that he'd never forget me. Each morning when he stands in front of the mirror to shave himself he'll see Mrabet, and he'll be full of hatred and he'll let his beard grow, and finally he'll become a goat. Amigo Stettner, I write to you out of my heart. Inch'Allah (God willing) some day, some year, we'll see each other. And we'll talk about thousands of things, and each one will interest the other, with a true interest. Things that a poor man can do, a rich man can't do. And whatever a rich man can do, so can a poor man. We're more alive and stronger, and braver in our minds, we poor men. A pure heart is the important thing for me. And nobody knows what is going to happen later on. We're looking now at all that is going on in the world. Adios, hasta Dios quiere. Much good luck to you and to all the friends.

Mohammed Mrabet

Casa Zugari, Calle Ajdir,
Merstakoche, Tangier,
Morocco.
9/xii/81

Dear Amigo Stettner:

Many salutations and embraces. Again I ask your pardon for not having written. It was impossible in London, and you know I can't write any European language. I thought of writing you in Arabic, and then I thought nobody where you are would be able to read it and translate it for you. I stayed a little more than a month in England, and saw the doctor. And I had the operation, and all went well. After a few months I'll have to go back and see the doctor again. I already have an appointment with him.

Amigo Stettner, I'm going to tell you something you'll find it hard to believe. I liked London better than any city I'd seen. I liked the climate and many parts of the city. I found Windsor Castle a great place to visit. And I liked the Zoo, full of animals. And most of all I liked the people, the Indians and the Pakistanis and the English. There I thought was the most civilized place I'd ever been in. How well they treat the poor people! They get good pay and live in good houses, and have everything they need. There's no difference between the black and the white people. They are all equal, and are all treated equally. All this struck me very hard, and made me think of many things. And it brought tears to my eyes, without my knowing it. There's no one there to be always annoying you and making you nervous and angry. Everybody smiles. It was all perfect for me, and all wonderful.

Amigo Stettner, adios. Hasta Dios quiere. Much luck to you and all your friends. I'll write you soon.

Mohammed Mrabet

(*Stroker 22*, between pages 12 and 13)   Tangier, Morocco
23/ii/82

Querido Amigo Stettner:

I send you many salutations and embraces. I ask your forgiveness and that of our dear friends for not having written you in a long time. But they mustn't blame me, because I have so little time these days. There is so much work to do in the country, planting all kinds of vegetables and trees, and now it rains heavily fairly often. (I don't believe it has rained so much in fifteen or twenty years. I mean all at once, and hard, as it has done this winter.) Everyone is happy with this, of course. If we hadn't had these rains, Morocco would have been in a terrible state. It would have been the way it was after the last World War, when people waited in line all night for bread. I remember very well how people used to pull out a loaf of bread from under their clothing and offer it for sale if no one was looking. And people had plenty of money, but it did them no good. But now there's no danger of that. This is a fortunate and happy year.

About my letters, if there are enough of them, you can make a book of them, yes. And if there aren't enough, I'll do everything I can to send more, so that there will be enough. Amigo Stettner, you must not imagine that I don't want to write to you. It's all the work I have to do, and when I finish with it, I'm very tired. I'm spending all my energy trying to finish this farm quickly. I think people will be coming to visit me out there at Mraier this summer, and I want to have it ready.

Amigo Stettner, I'm doing something which may seem strange for anyone to do. Someone arriving at my piece of land may find it unusual. But he'd like all of it, inside and outside. One morning early it rained very hard. The bottom of my land is a stream bed. I was working in the stream down there so the water would run where it should run. Then I saw a doll coming down the stream. It had arms and legs made of cane, and it was well dressed. At the same time I thought I heard a child screaming. I took the doll out of the water and began to run with it up the hill, maybe two hundred metres. There I found a little girl caught between two boulders while the water of the stream poured over her. The rain had made the stream very powerful. I jumped into the water and pulled the child out from between the rocks. I took all her clothes off and wrapped her in a woolen coat. Then I heard people coming, and it was the child's mother and the rest of the family. The mother looked at the little girl and said: "You're a donkey." And I said: "No, lalla, the child isn't a donkey. She's only four years old, and I think you're the cow. And if I weren't ashamed to do it, since we're neighbors, I'd take her with me to the moqqaddem, and the moqqaddem would take her to the khalifa, and the khalifa would come and punish you." I gave the woman her daughter and her daughter's doll. The sister of the mother said: "You see, my sister has thirteen children." And I said to her: "I see. That's why one doesn't matter to her. She's got enough more."

Amigo Stettner, when you come to Tangier, my house is yours, and good-bye. Hasta Dios quiere. Good luck and good health to you and to all our friends. Until soon,

Mohammed Mrabet

Casa Zugari, Calle Ajdir,
Merstakhoche, Tangier,
Morocco.
10/iii/82

Querido Amigo Stettner:

Many greetings and embraces for you and all our friends. Good afternoon. It is five minutes to six in the afternoon. I am going to begin something called <u>Kann Fkoul el Mkann</u>. A fisherman who fished only with a bamboo pole, married and with one son. Very poor. One day in March the boy came home and said to his mother: Can you give me half a real, yimma? She said to him: My son, I had three reales, and I spent one for our food today, and there are two left. Yesterday your father didn't bring any fish back. The sea was very bad. If he doesn't bring anything today, tomorrow I'll have to spend another real. Your father spent twelve hours fishing yesterday, and all he caught was an old teapot. And the boy said: And where is the teapot, yimma? It's over there in the corner, she told him. The boy went and picked up the teapot. Then he cleaned it, and filled it with water, and saw that it had no holes in it, so that all the water stayed inside. He went to his mother and said: And can you give me a little sugar and a little mint and some tea? The mother said: Yes, aoulidi. She gave him what he had asked for, and he put it all into a basket along with three little tea glasses, and went out of the house. It was a wonderful day, so he walked far from his house. Then he came upon a huge old olive tree that had been growing for many centuries. It was at the edge of a great property in the middle of which stood a castle. The boy gathered some pieces of wood and lit a fire. When it was burning he put the teapot on top so that the water would boil. And he sat down, leaning against the olive tree. When the water was boiling, he put the tea and the mint and the sugar into the teapot. But the smoke from the fire was blown by the wind to the windows of the castle, and a girl who was inside one of the rooms smelled it. She looked out the window, saw the boy sitting some distance away under the olive tree, and called one of her servants. Go and tell that boy to put his fire out and leave the premises, she told the girl. The servant went out to the boy. The lady in the house says to put the fire out and go away, she said. The boy's sebsi and his kif lay beside him on the ground. He looked at her and said: Yes. But wait a minute, please. Then he poured out some tea into two of the little glasses. Here, he said. One glass for you, and one glass for the lady in the house. The servant took the two glasses and went to the castle with them. When she had gone, he poured himself some tea into the third glass, put the fire out, and said to himself: I'll drink my tea, smoke a pipe of kif, and be on my way. He lifted the glass to his lips, but there was no tea. Then he stared at the glass, turned it upside down, and watched a tube of gold slide out of it and fall to the ground. He quickly gathered up everything, and went running away as fast as he could. The servant meanwhile went to the room where the girl was, with the two glasses in her hand. The girl cried: What's that you've got? Lalla, the boy gave me these two glasses of tea, one for you and one for me. The girl struck both glasses from the servant's hands, and they fell to the floor, smashed the glasses and leaving two small tubes of gold lying among the pieces of broken glass. Then the girl bent over and seized both pieces of gold in her hands and looked for a long time at them. And she looked at the servant girl and said to her: Run and find that boy, and tell him to come here and see me. The servant went out, and soon came back, saying that the boy was nowhere to be seen. If you ever see him again, bring him to me. What does he look like? He's very young, and he smokes kif, said the servant.

The boy went straight to the joteya, where he sold the piece of gold. Then he bought a great amount of food of all kinds, and carried everything home. He handed the basket to his mother. Where did this all come from? she demanded. I have very good work now, he told her. What sort of work? she wanted to know. I have a gold-smelting factory, he said. She did not understand, but she was very happy to hear of her son's work. She began to prepare the meal in the kitchen. Presently the fisherman came into the street, and smelled the odor of food cooking coming from his house. What a wonderful smell, he thought. One bowl of that soup would be enough for me. It's ten years since I tasted food that smelled like that. He did not know that the odor was coming from his own kitchen until he got to the door of his house. He went in, and when he saw all the food in the kitchen, he said to his wife: What's this?

Your son brought it, she told him. What? he cried. Is he earning money? Yes, she said. He says he's working in a gold factory.

Some time later the boy returned to the old olive tree near the castle. I'm going to build a fire, he thought, and then I'll find out what happened with those two glasses of tea. He sat down and began to smoke. Soon the servant girl caught sight of him, and she went and told her mistress that the boy was there. Go and tell him to come here, she said. The servant went to the olive tree. My mistress wants to speak with you, she told him, and he rose and went with her to the castle. She took him to the room where the girl was, and the girl said to her: You may leave us. When she had gone, they sat down. The first thing she said to him was: Why don't you give me your teapot? I see you're carrying it with you. He said: And what are you going to give me in return? Whatever you want, she said. The boy, who was looking at her with great interest, said: If I give you my teapot, we must make love together. As you like, said the girl, and they went to bed, and the girl became a woman at that moment. And the boy gave her the teapot along with an empty glass, saying: Glass! What a glass! But my glass is my glass, and he went out of the castle by himself, saying only those words.

And for a long time no one knew where he was, or whether he was alive or dead. His parents searched for him and could not find him.

Three months or so afterward, the servant girl saw that her mistress looked strange, and she decided that she was ill. She went to the girl's mother in another part of the castle. Lalla, your daughter looks very ill to me. Whatever she eats, she vomits up. What? cried the woman. She went down to see the girl and found her in bed. What's wrong, daughter? she asked her. Nothing, yimma, nothing, said the girl. No, you must tell me the truth, her mother insisted. Finally the girl said: The truth is that I have a child inside me. What! cried the woman. Yes, yimma, the girl said.

My daughter, wait until your father comes home tonight. He's going to kill you. The girl remained in her room. Later her father returned. He embraced his wife and daughter. They ate their dinner. When the man and woman retired to their chamber, the woman waited until her husband's passion was roused, and then she said to him: Something horrible has happened, but before I tell you what it is, you must promise me that you won't kill anyone. The man swore that he would kill nobody. They finished making love, and then she said: Your daughter has a child inside her. I'm going to kill her! he shouted. You swore you wouldn't, she reminded him. Then I'm going to throw her into the sea, he said.

He called in four workmen and had them bring a huge chest. The woman went to her daughter and told her: Take all your things and get ready to go. Your father's going to throw you out.

And the workmen dragged in the big coffer, stoutly made. Night had fallen. They packed all the girl's things inside the chest, and she got inside it, with the teapot in one hand and a glass in the other. Her mother saw this, and she said: Are you going to take along that teapot?

Yes, I am. Everything that happened is all the fault of this teapot. Her mother knew nothing of the special qualities of the teapot, and she did not understand. Do you think you're going to stay alive? she asked her.

If he's alive, I'll be alive, and I'll see you again, yimma, some day. They shut the chest and bound it well, and carried it to the edge of the sea. Then they heaved it into the water from a high cliff.

Very early one morning, the fisherman, who was fishing from the rocks, saw an object floating on the water. Something that has fallen overboard from some ship, he thought. He took off his clothes, dived into the water, and struggled with it until he had got it to a small beach. Then on the sand he began to try to open the chest. When he finally pried it open, he was astonished to see a girl inside. He leapt backwards, and cried: What are you? A demon or a person?

Sidi, I'm a person, and please help me, she said. My daughter, get out of the chest and come with me to my house. She got out, and they took all her things out as well, and carried them to the fisherman's house. There he presented the girl to his wife and explained how he happened to have brought her home.

They gave the girl the room where their son had slept before he had disappeared. She ate and rested a while. When she arose, she called to the fisherman. I have a little gold here, she told him. Take it out and sell it.

In this way they began a business together. The girl made the gold and the fisherman sold it, and they made a great deal of money. Then one day the girl told him to find the best masons he could find, and bring them to her. They came, and she explained that she wanted them to build her a palace, giving them all the details of how she wanted it, for it was to be exactly like the one where her parents lived.

One afternoon when the girl went into the kitchen, she found the fisherman's wife weeping. She herself was feeling pains in her belly, but she tried to comfort the woman. What is it? she asked her. Ah, my daughter, the woman said. I was only thinking of how we used to be, and how we are now.

I'm in great pain, said the girl, and I can't talk about it now.

The woman looked at the girl, and went to fetch two neighbor women, who came to the house and went into the room where the girl was. An hour later the child was born.

The fisherman and his wife wanted to give the little boy a name.

The only name this child is going to have is Berred, the girl told them.

One afternoon the girl and the woman were alone in the house, and the girl turned to the woman and said: I'd like to know why you were crying that day when the baby was born.

My girl, I had a son. He was fourteen years old, and he disappeared from sight, and I don't know where he is. The girl immediately asked her: And what did he take away with him?

He always went out with a teapot and some glasses, the woman said.

He's alive, the girl said. He's simply hidden away somewhere.

In time the palace nearby was finished. Then the girl filled it with exactly the same furnishings as her father had in his castle. She hired a large army. Then she sent half of her men to scour the land, looking for a boy who could only say: Glass! What a glass! But my glass is my glass. And in a small town they found one, with long hair, who said the same words, and they took him with them to the girl's palace. There he was taken directly into the baths, and they washed him and shaved him, and they dressed him and took him to see his father and his mother and the mother of his son.

And when he saw them, all he could say was: Glass! What a glass! But my glass is my glass.

The girl held the teapot in her hand. He saw it, took it from her, pressed it to his breast, and shut his eyes. A few instants later he opened them again. Then he saw his parents in front of him, and said: What's the matter, mother? Nothing, son, she said. He embraced her, and embraced his father. And he looked at the girl, and embraced her as well, although he was surprised to see her there.

And the child? he said. It's yours, she told him.

Then he went with his wife and son into a room where they sat down. And she told him everything that had happened.

What you must do now, he told her, is to invite your father here. She called a guard, and gave him a letter which she wrote. And she directed him to deliver it to her father. And tell him that the letter was sent by the order of Prince Berred.

In the morning they had several sheep slaughtered. And the slaves prepared all manner of fine dishes to eat. In the afternoon the girl's family arrived, but before that she disguised herself as a man, with serrouelles and turban. When they came into the presence of the girl and the boy, he presented her to them as Prince Berred. And they began a tour of the palace. The girl's father was astounded, and grew more astounded, when he saw that the palace identical with his own, down to the least detail. He said to his wife: We're in our own castle!

What is it? the Prince Berred asked them. Is something wrong?

No! No! It's a fantastic palace. We like it very much.

They were served dinner, and sat back to drink tea. Prince Berred turned to her father and said: I should like to ask you a question.

Yes, he said.

It seems you have a daughter. And now for a long time no one has seen her. What happened to her?

Yes, she's staying with some relatives in the country, he told her.

I imagine she's still travelling on the sea, she said. Because the boat she's in goes very slowly.

What! he cried.

That's the way it is, isn't it? she went on.

What nonsense you're talking!

The girl made a gesture to the old fisherman, and a moment later the chest was dragged into the room, and placed in front of her father and mother. Her father stared at it. What does this mean? he said.

In this chest two people were travelling, she said.

What two people?

Your daughter and the son she was carrying in her belly.

I only invited you to tell you the truth, she said.

I happen to have a great deal of power, and I can crush you all, he cried.

No, I'm stronger than you, she told him. And richer than you. You have two thousand soldiers working for you. I have twenty thousand.

Then she made another gesture to the old fisherman. He went out and returned with his wife, who was holding the baby in her arms. The girl took the baby from her, stood up, and ripped the turban from around her head so that her hair fell around her shoulders. I'm your daughter, she said, and this is my son. And that boy there is my husband.

Her father and mother walked out of the palace and went away. When they arrived back at their palace, her father took a scimitar and plunged it into his stomach.

Amigo Stettner, I send you all kinds of salutations and wishes for a long life. To you and our friends.

Mohammed Mrabet

Casa Zugari, Calle Ajdir,
Merstakhoche,
Tangier, Morocco.
20/viii/82

Dear Amigo Stettner:

Many hugs and kisses. And I hadn't forgotten you. But for more than six weeks Paul was extremely busy. Even the translation he was doing for me of a new book of stories had to be neglected. Day after day the house was full of American students. Some of them want to be writers of prose, some want to be poets, others are interested only in what happens around them here. They pay and come to Tangier, and they stay at the American School, and Paul has to go there to the school. I swear, amigo Stettner, I don't know what Paul is doing there. And when he comes back to the flat, it's full of Americans sixty years old. But this year it wasn't quite like that. Some of the students were interesting. In every group there are more stupid people than intelligent ones. Anyway, with all that, there was no time. If Paul doesn't have time, I tell you, I can't write to you, because by myself I can't write. If something happens to Paul and he no longer exists, yes, I can write you in Arabic, and you can find somebody to translate it for you.

Amigo Stettner, this week some seventy fowls of mine died. The man who takes care of the animals for me went to the market where they sell everything, including animals, bought some chicken-feed lying in a pile in the street, and when he went back to the farm he fed the chickens. Half an hour later he saw them falling over. I had some beautiful ducks, too, as well as various breeds of chickens. Amigo Stettner, the work I had taken a year to do disappeared in half an hour. It doesn't matter. Everything is good. Man goes ahead doing his work.

My house is nearly finished being built. It's not finished because I decided to take off the roof I had built, which was of metal, and replace it with a cement roof. I hope that next week they'll complete the roof, so the house will be built finally. This year I had some apples from my trees, and figs as well. I had a few grapes and melons.

I have two books ready, both of stories. Another book will come out soon in California. I'm still thinking of how I can get to New York, taking Paul along. It's difficult, because he doesn't want to go in a plane. He prefers ships to planes. If I should get there, I'll come by and visit you. And visit many friends. Who knows? When they're here in Tangier, they seem like great friends, and when they're over there in the United States, they may turn out to be crocodiles. Amigo Stettner, adios, hasta Dios quiere, with much good luck,

Mohammed Mrabet

P. S. The latest number of <u>Stroker</u> [23] pleased me very much, as well as pleasing many other people. This summer many who were here wanted to see and read <u>Stroker</u>. Many thanks.

M.M.

Casa Zugari, Calle Ajdir,
Merstakhoche, Tangier, Morocco.
4/1/83

Querido Amigo Stettner:

I send many greetings. Thank you for *Stroker 24*. And thank you for the photograph you published of Trantino. I like the number, and thousands of salutations to our friend Trantino. Soon everything will be fantastic for him. And we ask for him a great good luck and a long life. And good health, too.

Amigo Stettner, I made a trip recently. A book of mine was being published in Holland, and I was invited to go there and be present at the publication. They agreed to pay the plane fare aller-retour and all my expenses, and I would have to tell one story to the public in Amsterdam and one in Haarlem. So I went, and I stayed in Amsterdam in a hotel. And there all the others were poets, and the only one who wasn't a poet was Mrabet. One morning I was in the hotel bar drinking my coffee with my bread, with four other journalists. There were six or seven poets there, and another arrived, somebody I didn't know and had never seen in my life. The poets were saying: Ah, Yevtuchenko! And he began to speak in English, but he made the words suffer as he said them. And he had a newspaper in his hand, and he said: "This is supposed to be for poets, and they've invited this one." And he showed the paper to the other poet, and there was a big picture of me there. Another poet was sitting there, drinking beer and reading the paper. He was an American named Corso. He looked at the Russian and said: "Why not? Mrabet is one of the good writers. And he is a poet, too, but he doesn't realize it himself." Then he said to me: "When you go to Tangier, Mrabet, tell Paul Bowles I respect him. And I respect you, Mrabet. Don't forget we've been friends since 1961." I said: "It's true." The Russian came and shook hands with me. And he asked me a question: "You don't write, is that correct?" I said: "I can write a little, and I speak a little. I've noticed that poets don't like prose-writers." "They're not in agreement among themselves." He didn't want to go on talking about that, so he suddenly said: "Is Morocco still making war against the Polisario?" I said: "What Polisario? What's that? There is no such thing." He said: "Oh, against Algeria? I see." And I said: "Morocco isn't fighting either the Polisario or the Algerians."

"Well, then," he said, "who is she fighting?" "Morocco is fighting Russia," I told him. "What?!" he shouted. "That's right," I said. "And Morocco has plenty of new Russian arms that our soldiers have captured, and it's to keep us fighting for another twenty years." Yevtuchenko looked at me and his face was red. "It's strange that a Russian is allowed to get out of the USSR and go where he pleases." He looked at me with an angry eye, and walked away.

Amigo Stettner, I tell you the truth, I had a success in Amsterdam with my book and also talking before the public. The people of Holland were very friendly, and I liked them. And now I'm working. The house is all finished, and all that remains is to build a fireplace. This year the rains have been wonderful. Now we're having a season of hot sunshine. The air is chilly, but the sun makes up for it. I saw some Germans swimming in the Atlantic the other day. Amigo Stettner, I'm going to tell you a little story that happened long ago in New York. It's something Paul told me. A Cuban girl was working in the house of an American, and when she cleaned the house and began to dust the tables and bureaus, she would sing very loud and look around to see if anybody was watching, and then brush the things she wanted for herself off the tables into the waste basket along with the trash: silk stockings, fountain pens, creams and perfumes and cosmetics, whatever the people in the house had that she liked. Then she would carry the waste basket downstairs into the cellar, take out the things she wanted, and throw the rest away. One day she left the windows all open. These Americans had a drawing by Dali, showing Harpo Marx playing a harp strung with barbed wire, and giraffes on fire running in the desert behind. It was in a fine frame, just as Dali had given it to the American. The window was open, and the picture was on the desk beside the window. And it thundered and lightened and the wind blew and the rain came down and went inside the room, and fell on the drawing and ruined it. When the American came home, he saw the drawing and began to shout. He called: "Linda!" Linda came running, and he said: "Look at my picture! See what's happened to it." And the girl looked at the picture and looked at him, and said: "It's too bad. And it was such a lovely picture of your mother."

Amigo Stettner, many thanks, and good-bye, and good luck, and many salutations to our friends. And Happy New Year to everybody.

Mohammed Mrabet

Merstakhoche, Tangier, Morocco.
15/iii/83

Querido Amigo Stettner:

Saludos y recuerdos! To you and our friends. Thank you for your letter. Here in Tangier I'm working a good deal. I've made great quantities of drawings, and recorded many stories. Last month Paul was sick in bed for a long time, almost a month. Now he is feeling better, and is back to doing his work. What happened was that when he finally got out of bed he began to eat like a locust – that means everything – and now he looks well. Amigo Stettner, it's very sad about our great friend Tennessee Williams. The day he died Paul was sick in his bed, and he heard it from London on BBC. When I arrived Paul told me: Tennessee is dead. I began to laugh, because I didn't believe him. Because I knew Tennessee very well. He couldn't die – bam! like that. I said: If he's dead, somebody killed him. And the criminal wasn't someone he didn't know. It was someone very close to him. If they ever catch the man, they'll find there were many others along with him in his plan. Amigo Stettner, afterward I sat without saying anything for a long time, simply thinking about him. I was very fond of him, and to know he's dead makes me sad. Even though he was almost 72, he looked like a very healthy man. There won't be another Tennessee. Amigo Stettner, here in Tangier we have summer days sometimes. Much sun, everything green and many flowers, everything smells fantastic. The countryside looks very green and clean. Tourists and Moroccans bathing on the beach. And I'm working each day on my farm. Now I'm sowing many kinds of flowers. I need to have flowers, to be able to give them to my friends so they can put them on the graves of their relatives. So the dead bodies can smell roses. Adios, hasta Dios quiere, with much luck.

Mohammed Mrabet

(*Stroker 26-27*, Double Issue, page 24)   Casa Zugari, Calle Ajdir,
                                              Merstakhoches, Tangier,
                                              Morocco.
                                              8/viii/72

Querido amigo Stettner:

I send you many salutations. Thank you for sending me the copies of <u>Stroker #25</u>. Amigo Stettner, it's a long time since I've written you. For one thing, in the summer Paul has no time to write letters for me. If he isn't at the American School he's at home, and the place is full of students. And what students. I've seen students walking in the street looking like church bells as they move. Students of eighty years. Others who are almost five thousand years old. Like statues that have stood in the rain for centuries and have pieces chipped from them. How can I tell whether they are real or not? They don't look real. And of course Paul is still working, but I think this is the last week. Amigo Stettner, I earned a little money, and I thought I'd make a trip somewhere. Instead, I decided to buy a large piece of land next to my property in the country. Yes, amigo Stettner, I bought the land. And there I am, cutting down cactuses by the ton, trying to clear the land. I'm like a crocodile inside there, and burned black by the sun. These past two days there has been a bit of rain, with thunder and lightning. And today, Monday, the sun is so strong it takes your breath away. The two hundred and fifty beaches are full, my friend. This morning I took a student from the school to the beach. So many people were there that the sand was not to be seen. That particular beach is five kilometres long, and it was full of people. All the beaches were alike. Tourists from all over the world. You walk in the street, and in front of you see the sun dancing. Amigo Stettner, let us hope that this year it will rain heavily, so that the streets and beaches can be washed clean. It would disgust anybody to take off his clothes and lie down on the sand now. I've seen horrible things that I've never seen before. The skins of people coming off and water running out from underneath onto the sand. Ambulances that come and carry away people who are losing the skin from their arms and screaming. I don't know what it's about.

Amigo Stettner, I don't know whether you've seen my book, <u>The Chest</u>. Without Black Sparrow. I went to another publisher, Tombouctou Books. The man who runs it came here to Tangier with his wife, which is how I met him. It's a good publishing company. And I liked the book and its form more than the editions de luxe of Black Sparrow. In this world nobody is interested in luxury; he's interested in making a living. The only people who insist on luxury and success are the rich, who already have those things. Black Sparrow is a bird that has plenty, so it wants editions de luxe. I come from a poor family, and I've always been poor. I hate luxury; I'm very happy as I am.

Amigo Stettner, when I returned from the beach to my house, I made a pot of tea, took off my shoes and my trousers and my underwear, and took a bath. Then I put on a chamir that was all black. I sat down and began to smoke my pipe and drink my tea. There's a big window in front of where I sit. On the other side of the window are many trees. And mountains. I smoked the first and the third pipes and shut my eyes. In two minutes a heavy wind came up, and there was thunder and lightning. And trees were flying through the air, and the mountains were exploding. Then a great black bird flew down and lighted outside the window. It called to me three times and I opened my eyes. And there it was in front of me. What do you want? I asked it. And it said: Help me. I decided to help it, and I opened a little box and took out a piece of majoun and tossed it to the bird. It ate the first piece and the second piece. I asked it: Do you want more? No, it said. If I take any more I'll lose my mind. And I want to take you somewhere you've never been, and where nobody has ever been.

I picked up my pipe and my kif and a big glass of tea, and got up and sat on the bird's feet. And it began to fly, and we flew in the sky. After a while it flew lower and landed on top of a mountain that stuck out of the sea. I got down and began to walk around. I hadn't gone more than a kilometre before I saw people. Hola! I cried, and they answered: Hola! Welcome! We've been waiting for you for a long time. They took me with them inside a cave where there were many rooms and halls. We sat down and were given tea and food, and we began to smoke. I turned to the man next to me and said: Where am I? He replied: My friend, you're in the hidden world. What's the hidden world? I asked him. It's the country without a government and without a chief, he said. We're all chiefs here. We're all rich. We have no jails because nobody commits crimes. Do you like the idea of living that way?

Very much, I said. Then a girl came in carrying refreshments. She was very beautiful, and I stared at her. She noticed this, and looked at me. One of the men sitting there asked me: You like her? Yes, I told him. Then he said to the girl: You like him? And she said: Well, yes. Girl, he told her. Go and bring your gift. And she went and brought in a necklace the like of which nobody has ever seen, and she fastened it around my neck, and she kissed me between the eyes. And her father told me: You must return home and get the bridal gift and bring it here so you can be married. Good-bye. Good-bye.

I went back up to where the bird was waiting and sat down on its feet again. It flew until it reached my window. When I opened my eyes there was no bird in the window, the trees were still in their places and the mountains looked the same as always. I bent to pick up my pipe and had a great fright. It felt as though a heavy snake had wound itself around my neck. But when I looked down I saw that it was a necklace, the one which the girl had fastened around my neck.

Amigo Stettner, adios and good luck.

Mohammed Mrabet

Casa Zugari, Calle Ajdir
Merstakhoche
Tangier, Morocco
13/vii/84

Querido amigo Stettner:

Many greetings and embraces, to you and to our friends. Mr. Kaplan arrived, bringing me the manuscript and two letters from you. He gave me the letters and the book, and met Paul. He also met my publisher, Michael Wolfe, who is here in Tangier. He smoked with us, and seemed to be very happy. He came again yesterday and stayed with us, and then I drove him to his hotel and said to him: Buen viaje! He's going to Meknes, Fez and Marrakech.

Amigo Stettner, the first day when I had the collection of letters, Wolfe took it with him to his hotel. The next day he came with the manuscript and said: "I'm going to publish it." Paul read it, too, and made some corrections. And I write you this letter now, and Wolfe is going to write you afterward. That way you will be in contact with him. You can write to each other or even telephone, when Wolfe is back in the United States.

Amigo Stettner, for the past few months I haven't been able to do anything but cook, wash clothes, make the children's beds and so on. My wife at last has had the baby: a girl whose name is Aicha, very pretty, very blonde, and with blue eyes. She was born a month ago. And the doctors, with the help of God, saved her life. Because many doctors had told her: You can't have any more children.

Amigo Stettner, I'm happy she's alive, and can be at the side of her children. That way there will be less work for me. Amigo Stettner, I'm going to write to you very soon, and it will be a sad letter. I've even lost my soul, amigo Stettner.

adios, hasta Dios quiero,
much luck and fantastic health.

Mohammed Mrabet

Tangier, Morocco
1/viii/84

Querido Amigo Stettner:

    Good afternoon. I've been doing some training for sports today. And I feel very light and with a lot of spirit, so I sit down and write this letter to you. I'm smoking a few pipes as well, and drinking tea with lemon. And Paul is in front of me, wearing a red shirt with white and black stripes and black buttons, writing at the typewriter. I'm always happy to see him typing, because the machine looks like a toy to me. Amigo Stettner, it was a great blow to me to lose my land and house. There are people who think they have good friends. I'm one of them. I believe I have many friends. Yes, amigo Stettner, I worked very hard there for three years and spent the money I earned and that people had given me for the farm. When everything was perfect and ready, people came and offered me good money, but I told them the place wasn't for sale, it was for me. If I'd done all that work, it was so I could live there. Half of those people became my enemies when I wouldn't sell. I did nothing bad to anyone. Amigo Stettner and whoever hears this, they wanted to send me to jail for 20 years. One afternoon when I wasn't there, a Mercedes drove up with four men in it. Each pair was carrying a large sack between them. Forgive me, amigo Stettner, before that they poisoned my two dogs. They came into my orchard and there was nobody there, and no dogs to bark, for they were already dead. They hid one sack in the canebrake by the river, and left one beside the house, and then they went away. Not far away there were two farm women who saw everything, and they went and looked into the sacks. They were filled with kif, and the women carried them away with them. An hour later soldiers arrived and began to search everywhere on my land. But they found nothing. They also went away. Amigo Stettner, the husband of one of the women came to fetch me later, and asked me to go to his house with him. And when I saw all that, no word could get out of my mouth. And I was very much afraid. I didn't want to go to jail without having done anything. If I'd done something it would have been different. Two days later I sold everything, and lost four thousand dollars. I didn't make a profit, my friend; I lost money. And I was ill for several months. Everything was terrible, and everything disgusted me: my wife, my children, my friends, everything. Amigo

Stettner, Michael Wolfe says he has written to you about the book of letters, and he hopes you will answer him so he can plan on publishing it.

Amigo Stettner, that's my luck, and for me everything is perfect. Sad, but that doesn't matter. Good-bye, until soon, good luck and much good health, and many greetings to our friends.

Mohammed Mrabet

Tangier, Morocco
                                          11/v/86

Querido Amigo Stettner:

      I salute you with two hands, and three or four arms. And I thank you for the letters you wrote me and for <u>Stroker</u>. My story is a story, Amigo Stettner, I don't feel well, either in my head or my body. Sad, pains, and I can't sleep. And I don't eat the way I should. My wife has had three operations, and she is in the hospital while I take care of the children. She'd been sick for three months. When she got up, my son, who is 15, fell down at school and came home limping. And in the morning both his legs were paralyzed. His mother went back to bed, and I had to care for both of them. At half-past five each morning I had to be in the kitchen. I had to wake up the other children, get out clean clothing for them, serve them breakfast, serve my wife breakfast, and take something to my son. And at seven I take the two children to school. Then I go directly to Paul's house, get his breakfast and prepare his food for lunch and dinner, and say good-bye, until later or until tomorrow. Then I go to market and buy all the food, and then go home. The children come back from school, and everything is ready for their lunch.

      Amigo Stettner, for two months the best doctors were examining my son, and couldn't do anything for him. And thanks to God I had a little money saved up, which I was going to use to make a trip. I distributed it among the doctors for their work and also to pay for medicines. Finally nothing happened, and my son stayed there in bed. A friend of mine told me there was a man who lived in the country who might be able to help. The man came to the house, and gave my son massages, and chanted words over him. The second day the boy was able to stand up. The man came on three consecutive days, and then he went back to the country. In those three or four days my son was completely cured.

      Thus you can see, amigo Stettner, how things have been for me, and what my life has been like. Now it's I who am suffering. Good, every thing has happened, and everything has come out all right, thanks to God. I hope nothing else bad happens. And now I am making a book once again. It wasn't I who didn't want to write to you; it was that I couldn't. There was no time. I wasn't thinking of letters. Even the book I promised to send to the publisher in America didn't get finished, so I couldn't send it. Now, I can write to my friends, and also finish my work.

Amigo Stettner, many salutations to our friend Trantino. Things did not happen the way I thought they would. I wanted to go to New York, and you would go with me to visit Trantino. And afterward I wanted to go on to Mexico. Well, another time.

Good-bye, and hasta Dios quiere, and much good luck to you and to our friends.

Mohammed Mrabet

Irving Stettner (November 7, 1922 - January 16, 2004)

A limited number of *Stroker* back issues, as well as books and watercolors by Irving Stettner, are still available from his wife, Mihoko Kato Stettner. Information can be found at the Stroker Press website:

strokerpress.com

CPSIA information can be obtained at www.ICGtesting.com
Printed in the USA
LVOW022322120213

319791LV00011B/293/P

9 780974 652757